OCCASIONAL
PAPER

From Flood Control to Integrated Water Resource Management

Lessons for the Gulf Coast from Flooding in Other Places in the Last Sixty Years

James P. Kahan, Mengjie Wu,

Sara Hajiamiri, Debra Knopman

RAND GULF STATES POLICY INSTITUTE

The research described in this report results from the RAND Corporation's continuing program of self-initiated research. Support for such research is provided, in part, by donors and by the independent research development provisions of RAND's contracts for the operation of its U.S. Department of Defense federally funded research and development centers. This research was conducted under the auspices of the Environment, Energy, and Economic Development Program (EEED) within RAND Infrastructure, Safety, and Environment (ISE). This report is being released jointly by EEED and by the RAND Gulf States Policy Institute (RGSPI).

Library of Congress Cataloging-in-Publication Data

Kahan, James P.
   From flood control to integrated water resource management : lessons for the Gulf Coast from flooding in other places in the last sixty years / James P. Kahan ... [et al.].
      p. cm.
   Includes bibliographical references.
   ISBN-13: 978-0-8330-3984-2 (pbk. : alk. paper)
      1. Floods—Case studies. 2. Emergency management—Case studies. 3. Disaster relief—Case studies.
   I. Title.

HV609.K34 2006
363.34'936—dc22

2006017783

The RAND Corporation is a nonprofit research organization providing objective analysis and effective solutions that address the challenges facing the public and private sectors around the world. RAND's publications do not necessarily reflect the opinions of its research clients and sponsors.

RAND® is a registered trademark.

Published 2006 by the RAND Corporation
1776 Main Street, P.O. Box 2138, Santa Monica, CA 90407-2138
1200 South Hayes Street, Arlington, VA 22202-5050
4570 Fifth Avenue, Suite 600, Pittsburgh, PA 15213
RAND URL: http://www.rand.org/
To order RAND documents or to obtain additional information, contact
Distribution Services: Telephone: (310) 451-7002;
Fax: (310) 451-6915; Email: order@rand.org

Preface

The loss of life and devastation in the Gulf Coast region of the United States following the hurricane season of 2005 have led to considerable debate about what should be done and not done in recovering from the damage. This paper reports the experiences of recovery from four major floods since 1948, to see whether there are lessons from these experiences that might apply to the Gulf Coast recovery effort. The cases are

- Vanport, Oregon, where the Columbia River broke through a protective dike on 30 May 1948
- The Dutch province of Zeeland, where high tides and a huge storm overwhelmed the sea defenses on 31 January 1953
- The upper Mississippi River region, where extensive river flooding occurred during the summer of 1993
- The Yangtze River in China, where extensive river flooding occurred during the summer of 1998.

For each of these cases, we examine the steps taken—both before and after the event—in detection, preparation, first-line response, reconstruction, and compensation.

This occasional paper results from the RAND Corporation's continuing program of self-initiated research. Support for such research is provided, in part, by the generosity of RAND's donors and by the fees earned on client-funded research.

The paper should be of interest to decisionmakers and other leaders in the region and in Washington who are grappling with the problem of recovery from the Gulf Coast flooding of 2005, as well as individuals interested in short- and long-term water management policy and the historical evolution of such policy.

The RAND Environment, Energy, and Economic Development Program

This research was conducted under the auspices of the Environment, Energy, and Economic Development Program (EEED) within the RAND Infrastructure, Safety, and Environment Division (ISE). The mission of RAND ISE is to improve the development, operation, use, and protection of society's essential physical assets and natural resources and to enhance the related social assets of safety and security of individuals in transit and in their workplaces and communities. The EEED research portfolio addresses environmental quality and regulation, energy resources and systems, water resources and systems, climate, natural hazards and disasters, and economic development—both domestically and internationally. EEED research is conducted for government, foundations, and the private sector.

Questions or comments about this paper should be sent to the project leader, James P. Kahan (james_kahan@rand.org). Information about the Environment, Energy, and Economic Development Program is available online at http://www.rand.org/ise/environ. Inquiries about EEED projects should be sent to

Michael A. Toman, Director
Environment, Energy, and Economic Development Program
RAND ISE
RAND Corporation
1200 South Hayes Street
Arlington VA 22202-5050
703-413-1100, x5189
ise@rand.org

The RAND Gulf States Policy Institute

The RAND Gulf States Policy Institute (RGSPI) is a collaboration among RAND and seven Gulf universities (Jackson State University, Tulane University, Tuskegee University, University of New Orleans, University of South Alabama, University of Southern Mississippi, and Xavier University) to develop a long-term vision and strategy to help build a better future for Louisiana, Mississippi, and Alabama in the wake of Hurricanes Katrina and Rita. The Institute's mission is to support a safer, more equitable, and more prosperous future for the Gulf States region by providing officials from the government, nonprofit, and the private sectors with relevant policy analysis of the highest caliber.

RGSPI is housed at the RAND Corporation, an international nonprofit research organization with a reputation for rigorous and objective analysis and effective solutions.

For additional information about the RAND Gulf States Policy Institute, contact its director:

George Penick
RAND Gulf States Policy Institute
P.O. Box 3788
Jackson, MS 39207
601-797-2499
George_Penick@rand.org

A profile of RGSPI can be found at http://www.rand.org/about/katrina.html. More information about RAND is available on our Web site at http://www.rand.org.

Contents

Figures and Tables

Figures

Tables

Summary

Introduction

This occasional paper presents a historical analysis intended to seek insights that might guide current reconstruction efforts in the Gulf of Mexico coastal region of the United States in the aftermath of Hurricane Katrina, which struck in the late summer of 2005. Katrina—and the failure of multiple levees in New Orleans stressed by the storm's surges—brought unprecedented death and destruction over a 90,000-square-mile area. As of this writing (June 2006), many area residents who evacuated before the storm have not yet returned. The social infrastructure will require significant repair and renovation. There is much work to be done.

In this paper, we examine four mid- to late-20th-century cases of severe flooding to observe whether and how lessons were incorporated into water management, both before and after the disaster (see Table S.1). In each of the four cases, the areas involved were subject to record rainfall or storms that overwhelmed the systems that had been designed to cope with these events.

Table S.1
Characteristics of the Four Cases

Case	Date	Geographic Location	Type of Catastrophe	Population of Affected Area (thousands)	Lives Lost	Economic Damage (US $ millions)
Vanport	30 May 1948	Columbia River near Portland, Oregon, United States	Failure of enclosing dike during river flood	20	15–32[a]	100
Zeeland	31 January 1953	Southwest part of the Netherlands	Storm surge overwhelms sea defenses	300	1,835	800–1,100[a]
Mississippi	June to August 1993	Upper Mississippi River, United States	River flood overwhelms levee system	64,000	47–52[a]	16,000
Yangtze	June to August 1998	Yangtze River basin, China	Severe river flood exceeds defenses	71,140	1,562	20,500

[a] Number varies depending on source.

We cast our examination within a seven-step analytic framework that is based on a *cycle of restoration*, as illustrated in Figure S.1. The cycle may be roughly divided into three stages: (1) *anticipation* of the next possible flooding event, (2) the *actuality* of the event, and (3) the *aftermath*.

- **Planning.** Before an event threatens, there should be planning about what to do when the next event comes.
- **Detection.** An ongoing information-gathering system is required, to provide warning of when and where an event will take place and also to monitor prevention and mitigation systems.
- **Preparation.** When an event is imminent, preparation should intensify. Lines of communication must be put in place, needed resources marshaled, and evacuation and other contingency plans set in motion.
- **First response.** Once the event has occurred, the negative consequences can be minimized by prompt and appropriate action to save lives; provide food, shelter, and clothing to survivors; and prevent further damage to property.
- **Reconstruction.** After the event has passed, rebuilding can begin. With the passage of time, decisions can be made about the extent to which the status quo ante can or should be restored.

Figure S.1
The Cycle of Restoration

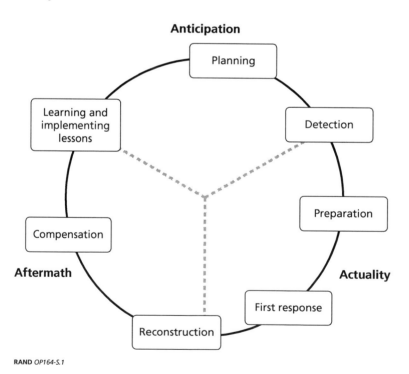

RAND OP164-S.1

- **Compensation.** Compensation, broadly defined to include public and private insurance payouts and other public assistance, is closely tied to reconstruction decisions. Where reconstruction is not completely possible or desirable, social insurance of some form can compensate individuals and businesses for their losses.
- **Learning and implementing lessons.** Finally, the experience of the event should be examined to understand the successes and failures and to apply the knowledge gained in anticipation of the start of the next cycle.

Lessons Learned from Four Cycles of Restoration

The four cases that we have examined are all illustrative of the evolution in thinking about flood management that has taken place in the past 60 years. All illustrate the evolution from flood control to integrated water resource management and the role of political, economic, environmental, and cultural factors alongside concerns about safety in reacting to the event.

Anticipation. In flood-prone regions, the question is not whether flooding will happen but when it will happen again.[1] Although modern technology, such as satellite weather observations and improved modeling of storms and rivers, has greatly increased our ability to detect emerging threats, our planning for an imminent threat is less consistently adequate. Especially when there is a long time between the previous flood and the imminent one, memories fade, training and readiness can become lax, and complacency among residents and public officials can set in. Financial and human resources that could be applied to readiness for low-probability, high-consequence events are instead pressed into service for what are perceived as more immediate problems—and then not replaced.

Actuality. Success at managing the actuality is in part a function of how well the anticipatory planning was carried out. Unfortunately, damage in major floods typically exceeds local and regional capabilities for prevention and mitigation, as was true in all of our cases.

First response, on the other hand, can be accomplished—within limits—independently of the magnitude of the flood. Even when local systems are overwhelmed, well-coordinated regional efforts guided by effective communication and situational awareness can mitigate the suffering. Although the amount of advanced planning differed considerably from case to case, first response was generally adequate in the four cases studied. Rescue operations minimized the number of lives lost, refugee centers were rapidly set up to provide food and shelter for the homeless, and social infrastructure to manage the health and safety needs of the victims was not a major shortcoming.

For three of the four cases (the Yangtze being the exception, because of the ability of the Chinese government to enforce—in this case benevolent—policies), steps other than first response in the actuality stage that should have been taken were not. Inadequate execution

---

[1] The ability of a measure to protect against a flood is generally expressed in the "design level" of the measure. The design level is based on engineers' estimates of the probability of flooding to an extent that will exceed protective capacity; it is expressed as a recurrence interval, say once in 100 years. The choice of design level (say, against a 100-year flood versus a 500-year flood) is a matter of policy, of balancing cost and risk.

ranged from the policy errors of ignoring warnings of inadequate protection and failing to have a response and rescue plan in place should flooding occur to the practical error of not ensuring that levees and dikes were adequately maintained. Moreover, even when post-disaster analyses led to clear recommendations, they were not always followed. In short, better preparation is almost always possible as experience is gained, but sometimes the leadership of a region is not organized or inclined to act on the knowledge gained.

Aftermath. The lessons learned from the cases we studied were varied and broad. The 1953 Zeeland case triggered a period of analysis and reconsideration of water management in the Netherlands that proceeds to the present day. From thinking in terms of building walls of protection, the Dutch moved to including environmental considerations, which necessitated technologically advanced flood control solutions that were produced at considerable expense. Yet further thinking contemplates giving more land back to the sea—a move that is contrary to a long Dutch tradition in the opposite direction. This move is not only under consideration but is presently being planned. The Mississippi case was extensively studied, and a number of strong recommendations were made. They have been unevenly implemented, however, and this implementation failure could be a factor in the extent of the 2005 damage in the Gulf Coast region. The Yangtze case provided a validation of earlier lessons learned and reinforced the convictions of Chinese water management planners. Finally, the Vanport case led to almost no lessons learned because the abandonment of the town eliminated any incentive to learn from past errors.

The lessons for the reconstruction step drawn from the case studies can be captured in the following points:

- *Building bigger and better flood protection works does not necessarily maximize safety.* Surrendering land to the water in the form of forgoing development of floodplains or actively removing formerly reclaimed land can lead to reduction in property loss and lives at risk.

- *Differing perceptions among residents and political leaders of the permanence and transience of the physical environment can create conflicts in deciding what to rebuild, what to modify, and what to leave as is.* In democratic societies, resolution of these differing viewpoints is best accomplished in an open political process—in particular, a broad public discussion about alternatives to the status quo ante. In that discussion, flood control should not be the only objective considered.

- *Some potential improvements to the status quo ante are not intuitively apparent or politically palatable.* In the absence of analysis, there is an inherent bias toward recreating what used to be. Regional leaders would do well to expend effort designing and analyzing a number of alternative policies following a flood disaster that could serve as a foundation for informed public debate and increased public awareness of the options and the tradeoffs.

- *Structural solutions are necessary but not sufficient.* Decisionmakers and the public tend to be overconfident about engineering solutions because the solutions appear to offer substantial protection along with economic development benefits. Residual risks always remain; indeed, they increase over time as the existence of flood works such as levees induces further development. Instead, decisionmakers need to choose structural elements that are compatible with nonstructural approaches intended to achieve other longer-term economic, environmental, and social objectives. Although this lesson has evolved in the past century from being implicit to being explicit, it is still salient as long as the Army Corps of Engineers continues to play a dominant role in flood management in the United States.

Compensation was not a major feature in the Zeeland and Yangtze cases and was a sore point that could not be resolved in the Vanport case. The Mississippi case provides the leading lesson, and produced strong recommendations in terms of who takes responsibility for risks and the relationship of insurance and government compensation after losses. These recommendations were not, however, fully implemented. The role of insurance remains an underappreciated tool in mitigation of losses from flood damage, particularly in the context of an increasing expectation of federal disaster assistance.

Lessons from History for the Aftermath of Katrina

As our examples show, Katrina and its aftermath, like many crises, present an opportunity to improve conditions that existed prior to the catastrophe.

In terms of *planning* and *preparation*, all the examples demonstrate to varying degrees the limits of planning when the natural disaster exceeds expectations. Government officials had anticipated catastrophic flooding in New Orleans from flooding and levee failures. Further, officials also were well aware of the connection between loss of Louisiana's coastal wetlands and reduction in the city's protection from storm surges. On the coasts of the Gulf of Mexico, storm surges had been anticipated, but not at the heights wrought by Katrina In the future, regional leaders should consider policies and plans that are more robust against a wider range of disaster scenarios.

Throughout the region, however, the biggest blind spot was the failure to anticipate the possibility of widespread regional breakdown in infrastructure and services and the disabling of first-response and public safety systems. Some activities, such as evacuation planning, simply cannot be implemented on the fly. Evacuation services for all segments of the population must be worked through in sufficient detail well in advance of the event. The fragility of many structures on the Gulf Coast, along with the fact that so many of them were built to out-of-date building codes, underscores another opportunity for improvement. Here, the lessons of history are that, while determining safety levels might be defensible on cost-benefit or IWRM bases, the planning for regional infrastructure and services must cover total catastrophic breakdown and must include secondary, contingency responses that can be invoked when primary responses are overwhelmed. In Zeeland, lack of such planning led to catastrophe, but in the Yangtze case, this planning was a major reason why loss was only a fraction of what had been suffered in previous floods.

At the federal level, much has already been published about the shortcomings of the Federal Emergency Management Agency (FEMA) and other agency planning efforts, particularly in developing logistics for deploying supplies and personnel in advance. Although scenario planning had been employed by FEMA, it will need to anticipate a wider range of scenarios in the future to fully prepare its staff for a wider range of catastrophic conditions in major metropolitan areas.

Detection of the storm itself was certainly adequate in the case of Katrina—as it was in the historical examples—but detection fell short in anticipating structural failures and collapse under the forces unleashed by the storm. In the case of New Orleans, as with Vanport, the Corps and the local levee districts had no monitoring equipment in place to detect structural weaknesses, soil anomalies, and impending failure. This shortcoming can be remedied through deployment of sensors on all structural features of the flood protection system.

The examples suggest that decisions about how to proceed with *reconstruction* in the affected areas are strongly influenced by the answer to the question of what the level of flood protection will be in the future. In the four cases we examined, this decision was intimately tied to the commitment of the affected population to restore their way of life to pre-disaster conditions, albeit with some accommodation to the natural hazard. The Vanport example offers one extreme: The community was temporary and residents' emotional ties to the place were weak. The Zeeland example is at the opposite end of the continuum: Wholesale abandonment of the flooded lands was simply not an option for a small country, although over time the Dutch became willing to give back some land to the sea in return for more security.

The areas affected by Katrina and its aftermath fall in between these two extremes. By and large, Gulf Coast residents feel a strong connection to these special places, and yet they do have choices of where to live within the United States in ways that the Dutch did not perceive that they had. This psychological difference casts the public decision about the appropriate level of flood protection in more complex terms.

This consideration raises the larger issue of how to deal with the long-term evacuee population we face in Katrina. Most instances of flooding are short-term in nature—in terms of how long it takes for the floodwaters to recede and how long it is before people can be back in their communities. But Katrina resulted in a situation where there is permanent or semi-permanent displacement. This is an entirely different class of problem, one that requires possibly pioneering thinking in the restoration of the Gulf region.

Investments in additional flood control and protective measures will depend on the density and magnitude of populations and property requiring protection, which in part depend on the investments themselves—the classic "chicken and egg" problem. Many Gulf Coast residents have already seized options to move elsewhere within the United States. Under these circumstances, estimates of population return and the quality of a range of locally provided public services become important determinants of the extent to which the federal government should rebuild preexisting levees and improve flood protection through other nonstructural means.

Finally, it is still too soon to tell the full story of compensation in the aftermath of Katrina. Preliminary analysis from FEMA shows that in areas of the disaster zone where it applied, compliance with the National Flood Insurance Program (NFIP) was relatively good. However, the program's coverage is incomplete in the flood-prone areas hit by Katrina. Beyond the limits of the NFIP, private insurers faced major losses in Katrina. They will likely support more robust flood protection measures, reforms in building codes, and enlightened land-use planning that will reduce their exposure in the future, assuming they choose to continue to serve the region. This issue is clearly an important area for future analysis and policy change.

Final Observations

We close with some final general observations that span the cycle of restoration.

- George Santayana (1905) said, "Those who cannot remember the past are condemned to repeat it." This has clearly been shown in our case studies. Attending to history leads to mitigating the potential damage of floods even when major floods are few and far between; ignoring history leads to even larger disasters. Whether the Gulf Coast region will adequately attend to its recent flooding history remains to be seen.
- The critical concept of integrated water resource management policy—particularly its implication that flood damage control includes conceding land to the water from time to time—is a psychologically difficult one. This problem goes well beyond flood control. In almost all areas of preventive policy, there are times when an excess of cure can be worse than the disease.
- Delineation of roles and responsibilities in advance shapes outcomes. As with any large-scale event, there were many different actors in each flood, including national governments, local governments, engineers, the private business sector, and communities. When the actors had well-defined and well-understood roles, things generally went well. However, when such definition and understanding were lacking, the consequences of the disaster were magnified. The flooding of New Orleans has shown that this lesson has yet to be fully absorbed for disasters in which local capacity is overwhelmed and the impacts are regional in scope.
- Out of tragedy can come opportunity. In each of the cases, improvements to the social and physical infrastructure in the reconstruction phase went beyond flood protection. This shows that disruption of the status quo can create political conditions for broader-based social and economic change that might otherwise have been delayed or might not have happened at all. It is still too soon to tell whether the latest cycle of restoration in the Gulf Coast region will lead upward or downward.

In sum, the cases provide a sufficiently diverse set of circumstances from which to draw useful similarities and contrasts to the current situation in the Gulf. While social, economic, environmental, and political conditions before the disaster provide the stage and the props for the post-disaster response and reconstruction efforts, the cases clearly show that the past need not be prologue.

Acknowledgments

The genesis of this paper was an idea of Jim Thomson (CEO of RAND) that a historical look at how people recovered from flood disasters might offer insights for how to recover from the Gulf Coast catastrophe. We thank Jim for the idea and his willingness to support this effort. We benefited from sharp, constructive reviews of an earlier draft by Jim Bigelow of RAND and Gerry Galloway of the Industrial College of the Armed Forces, National Defense University and formerly Executive Director of the Interagency Floodplain Management Review Committee that investigated the 1993 Mississippi flood. We also benefited from less extensive but valuable comments by George Penick, Jack Riley, and Mike Toman of RAND. Miriam Polon's editing improved the readability of the paper.

Abbreviations

Corps	U.S. Army Corps of Engineers
CWRC	Changjiang (Yangtze) Water Resource Commission (China)
EEED	Environment, Energy, and Economic Development Program (RAND Corporation)
FEMA	Federal Emergency Management Agency
IFMRC	Interagency Floodplain Management Review Committee
ISE	Infrastructure, Safety, and Environment Division (RAND Corporation)
IWRM	integrated water resource management
MWR	Ministry of Water Resources (China)
NFIRA	National Flood Insurance Reform Act of 1994
NFIP	National Flood Insurance Program
NWS	National Weather Service
RGSPI	RAND Gulf States Policy Institute
RMB	Renminbi (Chinese currency)
USGS	U.S. Geological Survey

CHAPTER ONE

Introduction

A substantial portion of human history has been spent drying out after a wet natural disaster. Water is a necessary ingredient for life, much less human civilization. Harnessing water for drinking, agriculture, transportation, power, and recreation is the story of human history, but—as has been observed—every advantage has its disadvantage, and humankind is subject to the whims of nature in the form of severe storms, river flooding, tsunamis after earthquakes or volcanic eruptions, or erosion after extended extensive rainfall. Some water-related menaces are as regular as clockwork (such as the annual flooding of the Nile), and some are more rare (such as a statistically once-in-3,000-years river flood or storm), but virtually none are one-off events.

To Control or Not to Control

How to deal with waterborne problems is a key part of history. Many religions' stories of the beginning of the world tell of the world having a global inundation as one component, after which the world was rebuilt as a better place. Sometimes, humans just live with what nature provides, working around the disadvantages to exploit the advantages. Thus, the annual flooding of the Nile was an essential ingredient of Egyptian civilization; on a more banal level, surfers seek out extreme tidal effects for sport. Sometimes, people attempt to conquer nature. Dikes, dams, and ditches are all artifacts designed to change the natural course of water.

Over time, as technology became more sophisticated, human effort moved in the direction of attempting to control water. However, as our understanding of the physical and social consequences of control has improved, we have come to realize that sometimes well-intentioned efforts at control can make matters worse. In the past 60 years, there has been a clear evolution from thinking in terms of water control to thinking in terms of water management (e.g., Working Group, 2006). That is, because the forces of nature are so strong and because the side effects of human intervention are so complex, we cannot control water with complete certainty of outcomes. All too often, recovery after a disaster consists of attempting to restore the status quo ante, complete with its (all too often literally) fatal flaws. However, we know enough that we need not passively accept what water imposes on society. Instead, we can choose to prevent or mitigate the threats posed by nature—or even transform them into benefits—by judicious management of water resources and threats.

In the literature of addressing the threats and consequences of floods, this evolution has been expressed as a shift from a near-exclusive focus on structural ways of controlling floods (such as building dams, levees, and the like) to integrated water resource management (IWRM). IWRM policy takes into account

- *efficiency,* to make water resources go as far as possible
- *equity* in the allocation of water across different social and economic groups
- *environmental sustainability,* to protect the water resource base and associated eco-systems.

In an IWRM policy regime, safety is managed not only by structural measures but also by such nonstructural flood control systems as laws and regulations, administrative management and economic levers, and technical measures other than construction. Moreover, safety is only one aspect of water management; IWRM also seeks to balance environmental, economic, environmental, and cultural values. An integrated approach is increasingly recognized as a crucial support for structural systems in order to reap full benefits and achieve desired results from structures. It also provides risk management for flood control zones, especially in areas suffering from frequent flooding. Popular examples of nonstructural safety tools include zoning to prohibit development of floodplains and flood insurance requirements. More integrative systems include storm surge barriers instead of or in supplement to levees to provide environmental sustainability and economic development of floodplains. These types of measures incorporate the understanding that part of the time the plain will be under water.

The Cycle of Restoration

Reactions to an imminent or already occurring natural disaster can be categorized into a *cycle of restoration* of sometimes overlapping steps, more or less in sequence, as illustrated in Figure 1.1. The cycle may be roughly divided into three stages: (1) *anticipation* of the next possible flooding event; (2) the *actuality* of an event, from the awareness that the event is inevitable until the passing of the immediate crisis; and (3) the *aftermath,* both in terms of recuperation from the event and deciding what changes must be made to better anticipate the next event. We identify seven more-or-less ordered steps within the cycle, some of which cross the stages of anticipation, actuality, and aftermath.

- **Planning.** Before an event threatens, there should be planning about what to do when (not if) the next event comes. Such planning should include analyses of what types of threats might arise from an event; what can be done to prevent or mitigate those threats; how potential threats will be detected; and what sort of physical, organizational, and economic structures need to be put into place or made ready. Tools for planning include learning from past experiences (i.e., the previous cycles of restoration), collecting and analyzing information, training at multiple organizational levels, and making policy choices to influence public and private decisionmakers.

Figure 1.1
The Cycle of Restoration

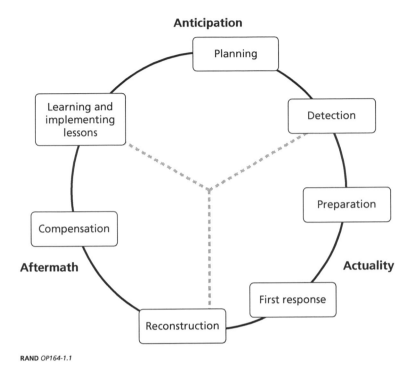

RAND OP164-1.1

- **Detection.** An ongoing information-gathering system is required, not only to provide warning of when and where an event will take place, its likelihood, and possible severity, but also to monitor prevention and mitigation systems to ensure that they are at planned levels. Information in an adequate detection system includes weather reports, measured rainfall, water levels on rivers, and the soundness of levees and the operating status of storm surge barriers.
- **Preparation.** When an event is imminent, preparation should begin in earnest. Lines of communication need to be put in place; resources that will be required must be marshaled, stockpiled, and made ready; evacuation and other contingency plans need to be set in motion; and preventive measures need to be implemented.
- **First response.** Once the event has occurred, the negative consequences can be minimized by prompt and appropriate action. No matter how well the planning and preparation has been done, there will be unexpected threats to deal with. Coordination of different agencies must be sustained, rapid reactions fostered, and ongoing monitoring of capabilities and actions maintained.
- **Reconstruction.** After the event has passed, rebuilding can begin, based on a triage analysis of where resources can most effectively be employed. With the passage of time, decisions can begin to be made about the extent to which the status quo ante can or should be restored.

- **Compensation.** Compensation, broadly defined to include public and private insurance payouts and other public assistance, is closely tied to reconstruction decisions. Where reconstruction is not completely possible or desirable, social insurance of some form can compensate victims for their losses. Organizational systems must be in place to provide this compensation in a fair and timely manner, according to standards of fairness that have—ideally—been established beforehand.
- **Learning and implementing lessons.** Finally, the experience of the event should be examined to see how better to plan for the next cycle. Recommendations should be based on both the strengths and weaknesses observed, and should address the physical/engineering, organizational, economic, and demographic features of the environment. Examples include redesigning the flood control system, designating certain areas as floodplains, moving all or parts of communities, establishing improved preparation and detection systems, and the like. The last step of a current cycle blends almost seamlessly into the first step of the next cycle.

Learning from Past Cycles

In this paper, we examine four examples of the cycle of restoration following a water-based catastrophe brought on by record rainfall or storm events that overwhelmed the flood control systems that had been designed to cope with these events. Two of the examples are old—over 50 years ago—and two are relatively recent—within the past 15 years. Two are American and two are foreign. All illustrate, in different ways, the evolution from flood control to integrated water resource management (if sometimes only by negative example); the influence of non-structural factors in safety considerations; and the role of political, economic, environmental, and cultural objectives alongside safety concerns in reacting to the event.

The four examples studied are, in chronological order:

- The Vanport, Oregon, disaster of 1948, in which a dike protecting the city from the Columbia River failed and the city was completely destroyed.
- The Zeeland, the Netherlands, disaster of 1953, in which an epic storm overwhelmed sea defenses, causing 1,835 deaths and extensive property damage.
- The upper Mississippi River floods of 1993, which caused 50 deaths and billions of dollars of damage.
- The Yangtze River, China, flood of 1998, which caused 1,562 deaths and extensive damage.

In Chapter Two, we look at each case separately; in Chapter Three, we synthesize the cases in the framework of the cycle of restoration. Finally, in Chapter Four, we look at these cases to learn lessons as the United States recovers from the recent catastrophe in the Gulf Coast region. This crisis is, like many, also an opportunity to do things better. Experience has shown that there are ways of thinking about the cycle of restoration that will lead to better anticipation and better handling of the actuality of the next event. Improvements in the form of changes to the status quo ante, which are often difficult to convince people to accept under normal circumstances, may be framed in ways that make them politically, culturally, and economically more acceptable. Although restoration in this sense is typically thought of as referring to land, infrastructure, and buildings, it can be more broadly construed to include education, health care, and employment.

CHAPTER TWO

Four Recent Historical Examples

For each of the examples, we first provide an overview of the event. We then discuss in turn the detection, preparation, first response, reconstruction, and compensation aspects of the cycle of restoration, ending with a summary of what we consider the significant observations. Within each element of the cycle and across elements, we focus on those parts that are most noteworthy and discuss what happened both before and after the event under consideration.

Table 2.1 provides some summary information comparing the date, geographical location, population of the affected area, lives lost, and economic damage of the four example sites.

Vanport

The Columbia River basin (Figure 2.1) is a complex, spatially broad, and heavily exploited system; its catchment area of 260,000 square miles and its length of 1,200 miles make it the

Table 2.1
Characteristics of the Four Cases

Case	Date	Geographic Location	Type of Catastrophe	Population of Affected Area (thousands)	Lives Lost	Economic Damage (US $ millions)
Vanport	30 May 1948	Columbia River near Portland, Oregon, United States	Failure of enclosing dike during river flood	20	15–32[a]	100
Zeeland	31 January 1953	Southwest part of the Netherlands	Storm surge overwhelms sea defenses	300	1,835	800–1,100[a]
Mississippi	June to August 1993	Upper Mississippi River, United States	River flood overwhelms levee system	64,000	47–52[a]	16,000
Yangtze	June to August 1998	Yangtze River basin, China	Severe river flood exceeds defenses	71,140	1,562	20,500

[a] Number varies depending on source.

Figure 2.1
The Columbia River Basin

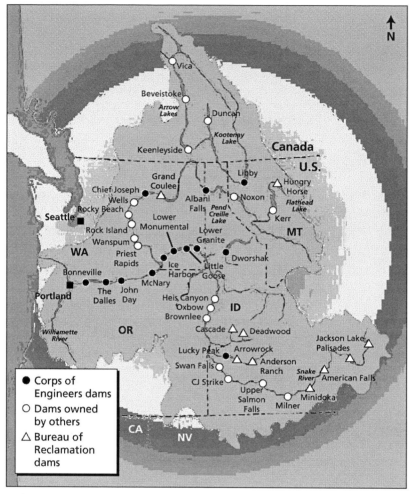

RAND *OP164-2.1*

most significant environmental force in the Pacific Northwest. It pours more water into the Pacific Ocean than any other river in North or South America. The river originates at the base of the Canadian Rockies in Southeastern British Columbia and enters the Pacific at Astoria, Oregon, and Ilwaco, Washington. The river is snow-charged and therefore fluctuates seasonally in volume; 60 percent of natural runoff happens from May through July. The Columbia has ten major tributaries, of which the Snake River is the longest, at 1,100 miles. The basin includes a diverse ecology that ranges from temperate rain forests to semi-arid plateaus, with precipitation levels ranging from 6 to over 100 inches per year.

Humans have lived along the Columbia River for more than 10,000 years, hunting and fishing in its rich waters. European settlers began developing the basin in the 19th century. Engineering projects on the river began with navigation canals at Cascade Locks in 1896. Extensive dam building during the 20th century resulted in 11 dams on the main stream by 1975, with many additional ones on major tributaries. The Columbia River basin is the most developed hydroelectric river system in the world, and the electricity generated by its plants has stimulated significant industrial growth in the Pacific Northwest since well before World War II (Bonneville Power Administration, 2001). Engineering works have dramatically altered the Columbia, so much so that some observers now believe that the river is environmentally threatened and that drastic action should be taken to reverse the changes made to it (Faber, 1997).

One of the most destructive floods of the Columbia occurred in May 1948. After a winter of heavy snowfall, the spring flood exceeded the capacity of the river, even with the extensive flood control system that was already in place. Although some damage occurred all along the river, the worst of the damage was the destruction of Vanport, Oregon, on Memorial Day (May 30), following a breach of one of the dikes protecting it from the Columbia.

Vanport was a community on the floodplain of the Columbia River, adjacent to the city of Portland (Maben, 1987; University Park Community Center, no date). It was built in nine months during 1942–1943 as wartime public housing for shipbuilding workers who migrated to the area to work at the Oregon Shipbuilding Corporation constructing Liberty ships. At its peak in January 1945, Vanport housed well over 40,000 people, making it the second largest community in Oregon, after next-door neighbor Portland. With the end of the war and the closing of the shipbuilding works, there was talk of razing Vanport, but it found a new life as an educational center, largely for veterans obtaining a college degree under the GI Bill, with a relatively stable population of 26,000. With the breach of the dike, Vanport was completely inundated, never to be rebuilt (Center for Columbia River History, no date; George, Washington, and McGregor, 2005; Maben, 1987; Towle, no date) (see Figure 2.2). Today, the site is a riverside recreational area in north Portland.

Anticipation

Although the Columbia River was, even in 1948, one of the most heavily managed rivers in the United States, planning for floods was mostly perfunctory and entirely structural in nature.

Responsibility for safety was largely in the hands of the Army Corps of Engineers (the Corps), which relied on the system of dams, floodplains, and levees. Generally, the Corps had confidence in the dikes surrounding Vanport, and indeed, the dikes would have been high enough to contain the peak flood levels—even in the extraordinary flood year of 1948. Part of the reason for complacency was the extensive control of the Columbia as much for commercial purposes as for flood protection (Bonneville Power Administration, 2001; no date). Historically, the two priorities for coordinated management of the Columbia River system have been electricity generation and flood control. Other priorities, such as irrigation, navigation, and recreation, are largely carried out within the context of meeting these needs.

Although the river level was caefully monitored and was at near-record-high levels, systems were not in place to detect the soundness of the levees protecting Vanport. Thus, in spite of regular inspections of the *level* of the protective structures, there was—as discovered after the fact—inadequate monitoring of the structural *soundness* of the levees, and that was the proximate cause of the disaster.

Figure 2.2
Flooding at Vanport, Oregon

SOURCE: U.S. Army Corps of Engineers.
RAND OP164-2.2

Actuality

Vanport was flooded because the dike area that was the oldest and considered the most secure collapsed because of a rotting wooden inner structure—and the water broke through quickly. This dike area was originally part of a railroad right-of-way and predated the construction of Vanport by decades. Responsibility for this dike section lay not with the Corps but with the railroad. That the demands on this protective dike would increase with the construction of Vanport apparently did not occur to anybody. In retrospect, there was a general consensus that it would have been difficult to detect this weakness beforehand (American Red Cross, 1948; George, Washington, and McGregor, 2005; Maben, 1987).

Because the flooding of Vanport was not believed likely, few preparatory steps appear to have been taken, and no systematic program for mitigation was in place. Although discussions had been held about ordering evacuation and preparing emergency housing, no concrete plans to do so were made (George, Washington, and McGregor, 2005; Maben, 1987). Vanport residents were repeatedly reassured that there was no cause for worry, and even the morning bulletin delivered to every household 12 hours before the disaster strongly stated that there was nothing to fear. When the dike broke, the city was flooded in a very short amount of time. Originally, it was feared that hundreds of people had lost their lives, but the final death toll was much lower—with best estimates ranging from 13 found bodies to an officially reported total of 32 if all the missing people never found are presumed to have died; the relatively low death toll was attributed by some to the fact that the day was a sunny holiday and many people were away from home.

Because of the absence of warning time, residents were forced to flee without any of their property. Although there had been no official plans for first response, the Portland Transit

Company was quickly able to mobilize buses to transport Vanporters to hastily-set-up shelters in the city, and the citizenry responded to the victims generously (American Red Cross, 1948; Maben, 1987; George, Washington, and McGregor, 2005).

Aftermath

The remarkable aspect of Vanport, and the one that makes this case worthy of study, is that it was not rebuilt. There was an ambivalence toward the community throughout its entire brief existence, brought on by a number of factors (Maben, 1987; University Park Community Center, no date):

- Vanport was built to house immigrants to the area, and Oregon has had a historic antipathy toward newcomers.
- The governance of Vanport was unique, to say the least (Maben, 1987). The city was built as a federal housing project, and the government owned all the buildings and their contents. Residents rented their apartments from the government at a rental rate considerably less than the open market in Portland. Although Vanport was carefully separated from Portland and was never officially incorporated or annexed, the Housing Authority of Portland exercised governing authority over the community.
- A considerable number of the newcomers were black, and although the housing was nominally not segregated, de facto black neighborhoods within Vanport were the rule. Although Vanport did not have the Jim Crow discrimination of the South, the Portland community was very nervous about the presence of this large community. Tensions were evident and open, although there was never any overt violence (George, Washington, and McGregor, 2005).
- Given the discomfort with Vanport's having been built in the first place, the costs of restoration, a postwar distaste for public housing as opposed to private construction, and a general disinclination to rebuild what was originally potentially temporary housing, nobody stepped forward to rebuild. The decision was made to demolish what remained of Vanport.

With no interest groups to champion reconstruction, either to the status quo ante or to renovation, the recovery effort was limited to cleaning up the detritus of flooding. The educational center previously located at Vanport, possibly the stakeholder most likely to assert a need for reconstruction, moved instead to the center of Portland and eventually became Portland State University, a largely commuter institution that is now part of the Oregon University System. The site of Vanport remained vacant. Over the years, the area between Portland and Vanport was gradually built up and annexed to Portland, and this created an impetus to use the land for recreational purposes. A park was developed on the site, featuring a golf course and other recreational facilities, and it was opened to the public in 1973. The park has become a major recreational center for the city.

The major issue, once reconstruction was out of the question, was what to do with the former Vanporters. Many of them just moved on, but a substantial proportion stayed in Portland and were gradually absorbed into the community (George, Washington, and McGregor, 2005;

Maben, 1987; University Park Community Center, no date). This included the black population, who—although not gladly received—did not suffer discrimination greater than what was typical in Northern cities at that time (George, Washington, and McGregor, 2005).

Because Vanport was federal property, there were no issues of compensation for real estate or building losses. However, the individual property of the residents was largely uninsured. Lawsuits against the Army Corps of Engineers and the Housing Authority of Portland were not successful, and so the losses were absorbed by the individuals (Maben, 1987; Monteverde, 1997).

Following the destruction of Vanport, there were the perfunctory after-action analyses by the Corps and the Red Cross, but little was done in the way of attempting to assess what went wrong and how to prevent a repetition. Instead, the focus was on not letting the tragedy get in the way of the long-term exploitation of the Columbia River. A speech in Portland by President Truman (1948) shortly after the Vanport disaster is remarkable for its focus on the development of the Columbia for power, agriculture, and shipping but not on the need for safety reforms, much less preventing a reoccurrence of the flooding.

Observations

Vanport was in many ways a transient phenomenon and a representation of a changing America in the period of World War II and immediately afterward. Founded as part of the war effort, Vanport never had a history or a cultural tradition and was artificial from its very inception. Little thought was given to its permanence or to fitting it into the surrounding culture of the Pacific Northwest. For its entire existence, it remained starkly different from its surroundings. The governance of Vanport; its economic, physical, and social infrastructure; and its rapid growth and decline are all unique to its short existence. The destruction by flood can be viewed fatalistically—this tragedy solved a number of social problems (although at moderate human costs and substantial economic costs), and what grew out of it is clearly an improvement. The Portland recreational area that once was Vanport is environmentally modern and provides cultural and aesthetic value to the community. The settlement of the former Vanporters in Portland eventually resulted—not without tribulation—in greater diversity within the community. Vanport provides an early lesson that flood management by structural means alone is inadequate and that cultural factors unrelated to the threat of flooding play a large role in reactions to floods.

The threat of the Vanport flood was always regarded as low, and even today the event may be viewed as "accidental." Indeed, an understanding of the risks from engineering failures at the time of the Vanport flood lagged far behind hydrologic methods to estimate flood frequency. As a general matter, flood control on the Columbia River is reliable, and the contentious issues associated with the physical infrastructure of the river basin are much more centered on environmental and economic benefits and costs than on safety considerations. The overall strength of the postwar American economy greatly mitigated the Vanport disaster, and economic expansion provided the opportunity for the victims to create new lives. Thus, in the short term, the change resulting from the Vanport flood was inevitable; any other outcome is difficult to imagine.

As a case study, Vanport serves as a proof of principle that if the social, political, and cultural circumstances permit, the cycle of restoration need not be an attempt to restore the status quo ante but can instead be an impetus for going forward to achieve broader societal values.

Zeeland

Zeeland is the southwesternmost province of the Netherlands; it is a largely agricultural area that is open to the sea and cut by deltas of three different river systems (the Rhine, the Maas, and the Schelde). Most of the land lies below sea level, and dikes have protected the land from the sea for centuries. In the middle of the night of 31 January 1953, high spring tides combined with strong winds to create a huge North Sea storm that overwhelmed the southwestern quarter of the Netherlands (Deltawerken, no date [a]) (Figure 2.3). Almost all the province of Zeeland was flooded, some of it severely. There were 1,835 people who died; 72,000 were evacuated. Over 200,000 head of livestock drowned, thousands of buildings were destroyed, and large parts of Dutch farmlands were inundated (Ministry of Transport, Public Works and Water Management (2001); Deltawerken, no date [b]). The total economic loss was estimated at around 1.5 to 2.0 billion Dutch guilders (US $0.8–1.1 billion) (van Dantzig, 1956).

Anticipation

The history of the Netherlands is a history of a battle against water. In the western part of the country, much of the land is below sea level, and dikes are an intrinsic part of the Dutch landscape and folklore. Much of the land in that area is *polder* land—that is, land below the surrounding (sea, lake, or river) water surface level that has been set off from its parent body of water by dikes and drained—in earlier days by windmills. In times of war—dating from the beginnings of the Dutch nation through World War II—dikes were deliberately destroyed and polders were flooded to deny the enemy access (Deltawerken, no date [d]).

The period before the Zeeland flood was one of complacency in the region. The 1953 flood, coming soon after World War II, occurred at a time when severe housing and food shortages took priority over dike improvements (Deltawerken, no date [c]; van de Ven, 1992). This was true even as engineering marvels such as the enclosing dike between North Holland ("Noord Holland" in Figure 2.3) and Friesland shut off the Zuider Zee and turned it into a freshwater lake and polders large enough to constitute the new province of Flevoland. Several studies by the Department of Waterways and Public Works (Rijkswaterstaat) in the 1930s and 1940s showed that several dikes in Zeeland were very low and did not meet the safety requirement to withstand a high storm tide (Deltawerken, no date [c]; van de Ven, 1992). Despite these warnings, little was done to improve the conditions of the dikes, and the area was therefore vulnerable to a once-in-300-year event, such as what occurred in 1953.

Figure 2.3
The Netherlands

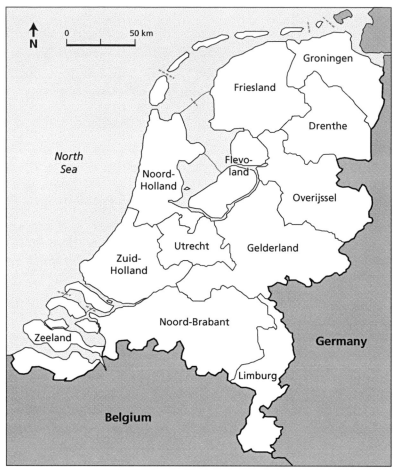

RAND *OP164-2.3*

Actuality

The flood itself caught people by surprise, largely because it happened during a Saturday night and Sunday morning. Although the high tide was known and the national weather service predicted the high winds, radio stations were not operating in this devoutly Protestant region and there was no other way of sounding a general alarm (Deltawerken, no date [d]; van de Ven, 1992).

Because the flood occurred in the night, many people were asleep and were caught by the water. With the dawn and a dropping of the water level because of abatement of the wind and low tide, search and rescue operations began in earnest. However, these efforts were disrupted by the next high tide and more flooding (Deltawerken, no date [d]). Within a week, an international rescue and assistance effort was mounted, which—although not without its own challenges—was successful by the standards of the day (Deltawerken, no date [b]). Once the safety of the survivors was ensured, work began on emergency dike repair and reconstruction. Recovery from the immediate effects of the flood took nearly a year.

Aftermath

The 1953 disaster was a major wakeup call to the Dutch, who resolved to prevent any future reoccurrence. By the end of the year, reconstruction had begun in earnest. The original major focus of reconstruction was rebuilding and improving the prevention system. For Zeeland, where there is no high ground, relocation was not an option (Verhagen, 2000), so efforts were directed at higher dikes, copying the model of the enclosing dike between North Holland and Friesland by walling off the sea. Immediately after the flood, the Delta Commission was formed to provide a plan for draining the flooded areas and protecting them from future floods to a once-in-4,000-year level (Ministry of Transport, Public Works and Water Management, 2000; 2001). The Delta Works project began in late 1953 and was officially completed in 1997, although thinking about and working on the project has not stopped. The full project has cost billions of dollars to date. A project like this was difficult to realize, because of both lack of experience and lack of funds, and the project was divided into phases going from small to large and from simple to complex, based on manpower availability and financial situation. Moreover, as described below, thinking about the most appropriate approach has evolved over the past 50 years.

The government of the Netherlands has traditionally compensated, on an ad hoc basis, individuals and firms that suffer from damage due to floods (Olsthoorn and Tol, 2001); this was the case in 1953. A more formal compensation and insurance system was put in place in 1998. This system is in part prevention, to stimulate less risky construction; in part an insurance plan; and in part an education system, to increase public awareness of the dangers associated with living in floodplains. As yet unresolved are the limits and requirements for insurance. One barrier to full implementation is that a single major event would bankrupt the Dutch insurance industry (Kok et al., 2002), and smaller events are largely not in the public eye.

The original Delta Works master plan followed Dutch tradition and consisted of dikes and blocking off tidal inlets. With time, however, objections were raised to the environmental, cultural, and economic consequences of this plan. Research led to alternative conceptualizations for protection that included the estimation of the effects on these other dimensions of value (Goeller et al., 1977). This led to a combination of dikes, dams, and storm surge barriers that were open except in times of severe storms. In this way, the restoration preserved the economic value of fisheries and mussel beds and the environmental qualities of the maritime ecology. The restoration was integrated with the prevention efforts, so that the region now not only preserves the agricultural and other features of Zeeland but is also a recreational and tourist area, not least because of the attractiveness of the technological innovations in constructing the storm surge barrier.

At present, all planned construction in the Delta area must assess the consequences of that construction on the safety, environmental, economic, and cultural characteristics of the region, as well as its effect on water. For the assessment of the effects of the proposal on water management, the operating principles are "retention, storage and drainage" and "not transferring the water problem downstream." If construction results in endangering the safety of the region or worsens water-related problems, the initiator of the construction will be liable (Ministry of Transport, Public Works and Water Management, 2000).

Thinking about the Delta region continues to this day. Although the Delta Works project was successful in meeting its original objective, new threats have emerged with time and increased knowledge. The land is sinking, the water level is rising, and the economic and social investment in the lowlands has increased; this implies more frequent flooding in the future that will have more severe consequences (Ministry of Transport, Public Works and Water Management, 2000). With recognition that traditional structural measures alone cannot deal with these threats, the Dutch created an updated version of the Delta Commission, which concluded in 2000 that new, integrated water resource management was needed (Dialogue on Water and Climate, 2002). In what is a remarkable revolution for the Dutch, this new group proposed not only spatial planning and land use measures but also that some land wrested from the sea be returned. In its new approach to integrated water management, it has planned to "give room to water." This principle is well implemented in the institutional structure of the Dutch spatial planning but not on the local policy level (Cooperative Program on Water and Climate, no date). The overriding rule is to hold, store, and then drain excess water. Certainly, it is not easy to find space for water in a small and densely populated country such as the Netherlands. However, the Dutch have tried to practice it as much as possible. For example, in the ABCDelfland project—a project launched by the water board of Delfland in 1998 that is redesigning the floodwater management system of Delfland to make it more sustainable and robust—several spatial planning methods are combined with the aim of providing more space for water. In this project, more space is allocated for multiple uses—water storage in times of flood but agrarian, natural, or recreational use at other times (Hoogheemraadschap van Delfland, 2006).

Observations

The remarkable feature of the Zeeland case is that a single event triggered a long-term dedication to rethinking water management that continues to the present day. The Dutch have historically been pioneers in reclaiming land from the sea, and they are now again at the frontier of water management in being willing to give land back to the sea in exchange for more protection from catastrophic loss and preservation of economic, environmental, and cultural assets. In a sense, they have had no choice; the country's very existence is at stake (Ministry of Transport, Public Works and Water Management, 2000). Nonetheless, along the way, they have integrated prevention and these other social values and have used technology development as a tool for an IWRM solution. The Dutch water managers, engineers, and workers learned a lot from their own cycle of restoration, and they now possess a type of knowledge and experience that they market today.

The Mississippi

During the summer of 1993, the upper Mississippi River experienced record floods. Nine Midwestern states—North Dakota, South Dakota, Nebraska, Kansas, Minnesota, Iowa, Missouri, Wisconsin, and Illinois—experienced major damage. More than 75 towns and millions of acres of farmlands disappeared under the floodwaters. Approximately 50 people died. Hundreds of levees built to protect the land failed. Thousands of homes were completely destroyed. Tens of thousands of people were temporary or permanently evacuated from the area (Witt, 2005). Damage estimates from the flood ranged from US $15 billion to $20 billion (U.S. Geological Survey, no date [a]). The area's infrastructure and businesses were severely affected (Changnon, 1996a; IFMRC, 1994; U.S. Geological Survey, no date [a]; Witt, 2005).

The mighty Mississippi River—originating at Lake Itasca, Minnesota, and discharging into the Gulf of Mexico at New Orleans, Louisiana—runs through most of the midwestern United States. Together with its major tributary, the Missouri River, it constitutes the longest river system in the world (Welkins, 1996), and its sub-basins encompass an area of 1.2 million square miles (3.2 million square kilometers), or 41 percent of the conterminous United States (Environmental Protection Agency, no date[a]). The upper Mississippi River basin (Figure 2.4)—running from its source at Lake Itasca, Minnesota, to its confluence with the Ohio River at Cairo, Illinois—comprises 57 percent of the total land area of the Mississippi River basin and 23 percent of the area of the contiguous United States (IFMRC, 1994).

Figure 2.4
The Upper Mississippi River Basin

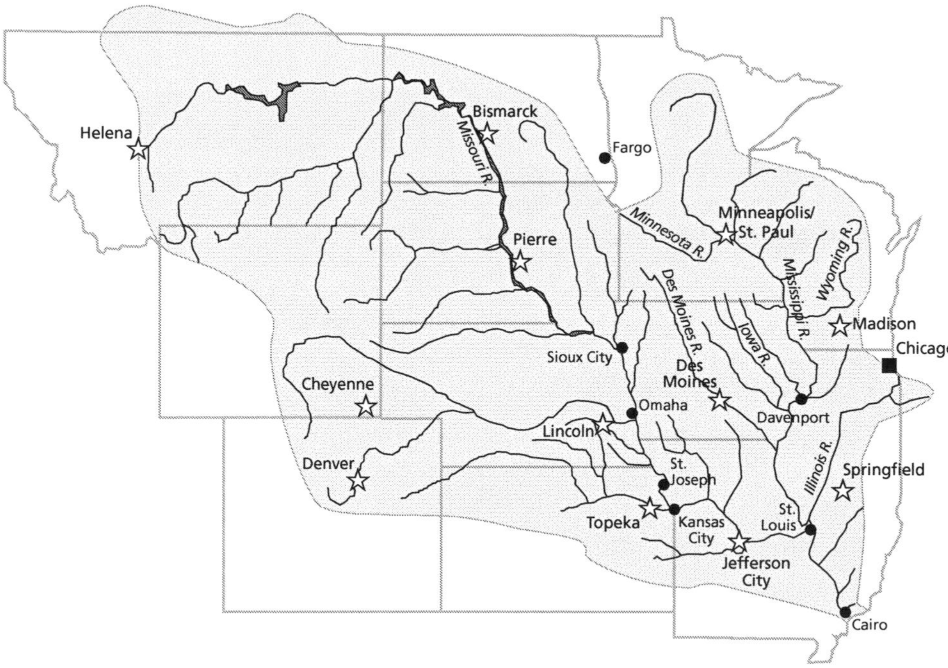

SOURCE: IFMRC (1994).
RAND *OP164-2.4*

Native Americans have lived in the upper, middle, and lower Mississippi basins for more than 1,000 years. They built their houses on relatively elevated lands, fished from the rivers, farmed on the floodplain, and used the floodplain resources as building materials. Flooding was part of their cycle of life, with few long-lasting consequences except for extreme events, in which case the survivors moved (Changnon, 1996c).

During the 18th and 19th centuries, European immigrants settled in the region (Barry, 1997; IFMRC, 1994). The first settlers were farmers, but urbanization slowly occurred as the river was used as a transportation system and as the area came to be used as a way station for development of the Great Plains. The newcomers changed the floodplain system by building levees and drainage systems to control the floods. In 1840—when the local governments of the lower Mississippi realized that they could not succeed in flood control by themselves, the federal government took on part of the responsibility. From 1840 to 1927, both local and federal governments followed a levee-only policy; millions of dollars were spent on constructing a levee system that was considered the best protection against Mississippi floods (Barry, 1997; Wright, 1996). This policy was severely tested in 1927, when some levees failed, others were blown up deliberately to stanch the flow, the lower Mississippi basin flooded, and 246 people died (Barry, 1997; Welkins, 1996). The federal government—especially the Army Corps of Engineers—was blamed for creating a false sense of security (Clement, 2001c). In response, major changes in the national floodplain management policy were made, including some nonstructural approaches to flood management. These changes stemmed from the work of Gilbert White and James Goddard in the late 1930s and early 1940s (IFMRC, 1994); however, the main defense against flooding remained the system of levees (Barry, 1997; Wright, 1996).

Anticipation

After the disillusionment with the levee-only policy brought on by the 1927 flood, consideration of nonstructural measures for preventing flood damage began (Barry, 1997). Some of these measures proved to be effective in the flood of 1993—for example, the relocation of the township of Prairie du Chien that was undertaken by the Corps and the nonstructural land management applications, such as wildlife refuges, that these measures provided for storage and conveyance of part of the 1993 floodwater (IFMRC, 1994). However, the Corps—with the full support of Congress—often only paid lip service to consideration of nonstructural measures. The rule remained to construct more and more levees; only some reservoirs and reserved floodplains were used.

During the 1993 flood, many of the locally constructed levees, as well as a few federally constructed and maintained levees, failed or were overtopped. However, many of the federally constructed levees, combined with upstream flood storage reservoirs, proved to be effective in reducing river stages and prevented potentially significant damages to large urban areas (IFMRC, 1994). After the flood, the Corps defended the effectiveness of its system of levees and estimated that it had prevented $19.1 billion in potential flood damages (U.S. Army Corps of Engineers, 1994). Critics countered that building levees led to more development than was justified in the floodplain, leading to the conclusion that reliance on levees can do more harm than good (*Economist*, 1993; McManamy, 1993a).

The National Weather Service (NWS) is tasked with preparing river flood forecasts and informing the public about the height of the flood crest and about the date, time, and duration of the expected flooding (U.S. Geological Survey, no date [b]). In 1993, the NWS worked with the U.S. Geological Survey (USGS) to collect and use recent hydrological data. USGS experts visited the stream-gauging stations in the flooded and flood-prone areas several times to measure river discharges and to check the instruments and repair them if necessary (USGS, no date [b]). The NWS, for its part, issued river flood warnings during the spring and summer of 1993. The information provided by both these agencies was used by the Corps—for example, to schedule reservoir releases; by FEMA—to reply to emergency need before, during, and after the flood; and by many state and local agencies dealing with flood management and mitigation (IFMRC, 1994; U.S. Geological Survey, no date [b]).

Evaluations of the quality of service provided by the NWS are controversial. Supporters believe that the small number of people who died in the flood is directly related to the early and accurate river flood forecasts (U.S. Geological Survey, no date [b]). Critics, however, believe that a large proportion of economic losses could have been prevented if the NWS had provided earlier and less optimistic warnings (Changnon, 1996a). They argue that, several times, the NWS made overly optimistic estimates that discouraged residents and businesses from taking proper preventive and mitigative actions. They claim that the models used to predict floods for the Mississippi and Missouri rivers were not reliable (Bhowmilk, 1996)—a claim the NWS does not deny. In its defense, the NWS argued that—computer model faults notwithstanding—the prediction inaccuracies were the result of some instruments being destroyed during the flood (Changnon, 1996a) and that many data collection stations in flood-prone areas had closed long before the flood because of insufficient financial support (Bhowmilk, 1996; U.S. Geological Survey, no date [b]).

After the flood, suggestions were made for improving the detection system by using more accurate technologies such as geographic information systems in data analysis and by using more accurate maps of floodplains—the outcome of the Federal Emergency Management Agency's (FEMA's) map modernization program (Cartwright, 2005). However, in spite of some improvement since 1993, detection along the Mississippi has continued to prove inadequate—as can be seen in serious floods such as the one along the lower Ohio River in March 1997, where existing systems for monitoring and forecasting were found to be inadequate and led to major errors in flood forecasts (Changnon, 2005).

Actuality

Prior to the 1993 flood, most communities in flood-prone areas had already developed mitigation plans, including flood-fighting operations and evacuation plans (U.S. Army Corps of Engineers, no date). Levees were supplemented with stockpiles of sandbags and other materials. In response to the flood, actions were often immediately taken to minimize harm. Evacuation was organized across official and unofficial jurisdictions, involving the Corps, National Guard troops, local officials, and volunteers. As official disaster areas were declared, FEMA opened several offices in the region to process applications for relief (Changnon, 1996a).

Communication was an important factor in successful mitigation during the 1993 flood. For example, many businesses had plans for informing their employees and clients during floods about the latest news to decrease their stress about what might happen to their monthly income, monthly rents, and insurances. Other firms donated cellular phones to city officials and to the Red Cross to improve communications. Daily newspapers listed resources ranging from temporary housing to child care services and were provided free of charge in refugee centers (Greenberg and Shell, 1993). Politicians reinforced the relief efforts with tours of the region and inspections.

At the peak of the flooding, all the transportation modes in the region were paralyzed. Considerable effort was expended to restore the operation of the transportation sector as soon as possible. River transport was the first to be abandoned, but the Coast Guard and Corps officials established a center to develop plans for quickly reconstituting service. The rail sector established "situation rooms" to deal with emerging problems and to restore operations. Road transportation officials engaged in a triage of damage, temporarily repairing highly critical segments and postponing permanent repairs because of the high soil moisture and the possibility of winter floods (Changnon, 1996b).

There were intensive mitigation efforts for the social infrastructure as well. Physicians, nurses, medical equipment, and supplies were immediately sent to the region, and the restoration and rebuilding of the primary health care services and systems was a high priority. A Midwest flood health and medical task force was formed through the Public Health Service's Office of Emergency Preparedness to deal with primary care, mental health, food safety, environmental health, disease control and surveillance, vector control, and public communication and information management (Axelrod et al., 1994).

Aftermath

Reconstruction after the flood was driven politically from the bottom up. Decisions to sell and relocate, rebuild, or do nothing were made by individuals, communities, and local governments (Changnon, 1996a). Among the options chosen (Associated Press, 2002; Hananel, 2005; Nixon, 2005; Taylor, 2001, 2003) were the following:

- Move an entire town to higher ground. This was done only in Valmeyer, Illinois.
- Relocate the most vulnerable parts of a town. Rhineland, Missouri, and Grafton, Illinois, were among the few places that did this.
- Elevate building foundations and change the interior design and building materials used in their structures. Darlington, Wisconsin, is an example of this choice.
- Partially rebuild and partially deliberately decrease a town's population. West Alton, Missouri, provides an example.
- Invest in new levee systems offering protection against once-in-500-year floods and further develop the floodplain. Chesterfield, Missouri (and to a large extent St. Louis and St. Charles counties in Missouri), chose this option.

Taken as a whole, development in Midwestern floodplains has continued to grow since 1993. Nonstructural options such as buyouts, wetland restoration, and insurance proportional to incurred risk have not been as extensively employed as was recommended. As one of the local newspapers noted in an editorial,

Apparently, we have learned nothing from the flood. Factories, warehouses, shopping malls and gambling casinos are being built on flood plains up and down the Missouri and Mississippi. . . . All this is going on with no real planning or region wide risk assessment. (*St. Louis Post-Dispatch,* 2004)

Following the 1993 flood, the federal government asked the Interagency Floodplain Management Review Committee (IFMRC, also known as the Galloway Commission after its chairman, Gerald Galloway) to provide advice on how to improve prevention (IFMRC, 1994; Galloway, 2005a). The IFRMC called for major changes in the structure of U.S. floodplain policy, including changes that would result in less development in the floodplains and changes that would increase individual responsibilities (Galloway, 2005a). In response, many agencies started to adopt more nonstructural floodplain management approaches, and the federal government decided to create policies to decrease the population living and working in areas at high risk of flood harm (Loven, 1998; Taylor, 2001). To this end, FEMA started a voluntary buyout program in which it offered to purchase damaged properties in the flood-prone areas to encourage the residents to relocate to higher ground (Clement, 2001a). However, critics found these programs to be too little and too late. For example, the FEMA program was viewed as failing to properly identify who should pay for the acquisitions and how and what properties should receive a purchase offer (Clement, 2001a).

The Corps, despite agreeing that the concept of "controlling" floods is outmoded and that more nonstructural measures should be incorporated in any flood management plan (Buss, 2005), advocated rebuilding the levees, in many places even higher than before, and Congress agreed (Taylor, 2001). However, Congress asked the Corps to improve the benefit-cost analyses of any project they approved and to increase the benefit-to-cost ratio used to justify a project from 1.0 to 1.5 (Clement, 2001b).

In congressional testimony more than a decade later, Gerald Galloway estimated that only 35 to 40 percent of the IFMRC's advice had been heeded. "The national response to the Flood of 1993 has been evolutionary not revolutionary," he wrote (Galloway, 2005a).

Prior to the 1993 flood, development and reclamation of wetlands for farming brought prosperity to the Midwest at the cost of higher flood risk. With the prospect of federal disaster relief in the form of supports and insurance subsidies, there was no real incentive to account for and internalize the risk (*Economist,* 1993). Following the flood, many federal agencies such as FEMA, the Small Business Administration, the Department of Housing and Urban Development, and the Economic Development Administration allocated funds to property buyouts, acquiring thousands of properties in nine Midwestern states (IFMRC, 1994).

For a long time, flood victims have been compensated through disaster relief paid from general federal government revenues, even though Congress has long recognized the absence of disincentives to redevelop in such an approach. Efforts to correct this situation are not new, dating at least from the time when the National Flood Insurance Program (NFIP) was originally enacted by Congress in 1968 (Dixon et al., 2006). NFIP did not establish actuarially rational insurance but instead allowed individual households to insure their properties in flood-prone areas voluntarily and at low, federally subsidized rates. However, the "take-up" for even subsidized insurance was small. Indeed, not carrying insurance did not expose the property owner to any further risk. In response, in 1973, Congress made participation in NFIP mandatory in selected areas. Even then, program participation rates were low relative to expectations (Dixon et al., 2006). Thus, in the flood of 1993, only a small part of the economic loss to property was insured (IFMRC, 1994).

After the flood, the mandatory part of NFIP was largely ignored, and federal funds were provided by many governmental agencies, such as the U.S. Department of Agriculture, to owners of uninsured flood-prone property (Changnon, 1996a). A total of $6.2 billion was ultimately paid by the federal government for flood aid, insurance, and loans following the 1993 Mississippi flood (Changnon, 1996c). As one of its conclusions, the IFMRC (1994) states that communities that chose not to participate in NFIP nonetheless received substantial disaster assistance, thereby creating a perception that purchasing flood insurance is not necessary. This has apparently contributed to low participation rates in the program. Therefore, the Galloway Report recommended that those who could have bought insurance but did not be excluded from federal assistance. Congress, however, did not implement this recommendation.

Compliance with the mandatory provisions of NFIP, however, would not have reduced federal spending. Because the 1993 flood was extreme—above the once-in-100-year predicted flooding frequency required for mandatory insurance—the federal outlay would still have been large even if these reforms had been in place.

After the flood, Congress enacted the National Flood Insurance Reform Act of 1994 (NFIRA) in a further effort to increase the participation rate in NFIP; this reform strengthened the mandatory purchase requirement (Dixon et al., 2006). This reform act was updated in subsequent years. Congress also lengthened the time for flood insurance to take effect from 5 to 30 days, to force households to buy insurance in advance and not to wait until the last moment, as happened during the 1993 flood (Galloway, 2005a). This reform established for the first time sanctions for those who do not comply with its provisions (DeClark, 1997). This legislation has been updated in subsequent years. However, federal funding for disaster relief, mostly grants and loans for rebuilding, continues to undermine expansion of insurance coverage (Dixon et al., 2006).

Observations

The flood of 1993 was a pivotal moment for the nation's flood management policy. It led to many changes in the way federal and local governments, engineers, regional planners, residents of floodplains, and the nation as whole think and react to flood management policies. Many policy issues were seriously discussed and debated, including the relative appropriateness of structural and nonstructural flood control measures, buyout policies, national flood insurance policies, and nature restoration.

The emerging perspective suggested that both structural and nonstructural measures be employed within an integrated approach—meaning that decisions should not be made for any structural or nonstructural measure alone but within the context of the management system as a whole. That said, the strong and reasonable recommendations of the IFMRC and others following the 1993 flood of the Mississippi River were not fully implemented, and costs were incurred from subsequent floods, such as those on the Ohio River in 1997 and the Gulf of Mexico in 2005, that might have been reduced.

Yangtze

Snaking its way over 3,900 miles from western China's Qinghai-Tibet Plateau to the East China Sea, the Yangtze (Changjiang) River stretches across ten provinces (Figure 2.5). The Yangtze River is the third-longest river in the world, originating in the Qinghai-Tibet Plateau at an average elevation of nearly 15,000 feet. It is the most important waterway linking the leading industrial and commercial hub, Shanghai, to its economic hinterland of the Yangtze River basin. The basin covers nearly 800,000 square miles, about one-fifth of China's territory, and provides a home for nearly 400 million people (Zong and Chen, 2000). The Yangtze River catchments have been divided into three "reaches." The upper reach runs mainly through mountainous regions with sudden rapids, whereas the middle and lower reaches are on alluvial plains. The Yangtze River is rich in water resources, with an annual discharge of about 34 trillion cubic feet, or 37 percent of the national total surface discharge (Li, 2000).

Development within the Yangtze basin has been threatened by floods throughout history. The first flood on written record in China dates back to 185 BC. In recent years, floods have occurred increasingly frequently. The most recent major flood, and the focus of this discussion,

Figure 2.5
China and the Yangtze River

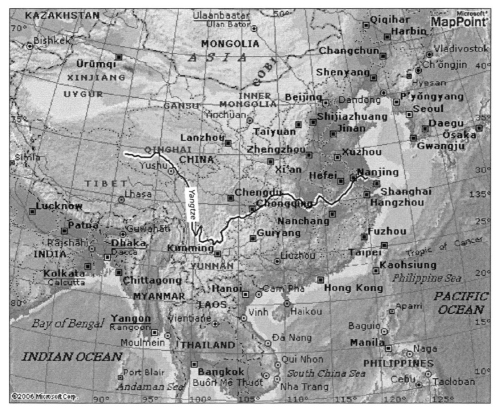

Figure 2.6
Affected Regions in the 1998 Yangtze Flood

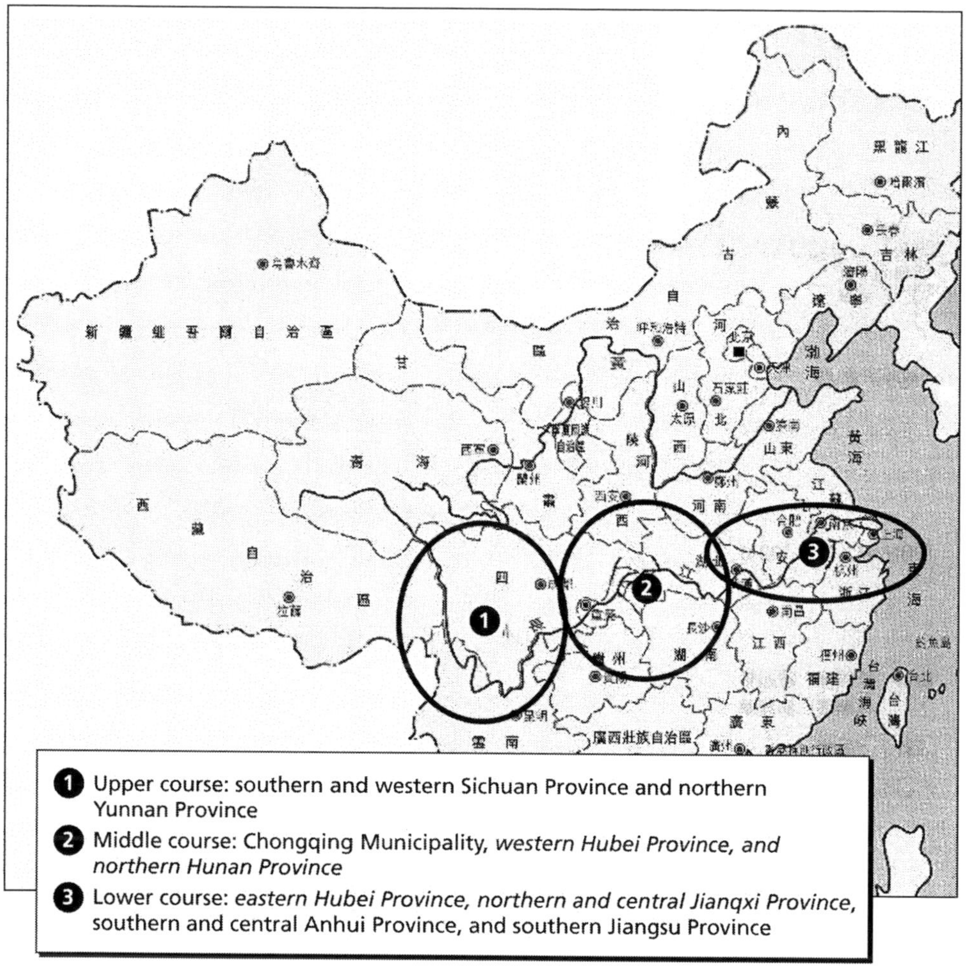

① Upper course: southern and western Sichuan Province and northern Yunnan Province
② Middle course: Chongqing Municipality, *western Hubei Province, and northern Hunan Province*
③ Lower course: *eastern Hubei Province, northern and central Jianqxi Province,* southern and central Anhui Province, and southern Jiangsu Province

NOTE: Italics denote most serious.
RAND OP164-2.6

occurred in 1998 (Figure 2.6); previous major 20th-century floods occurred in 1911 and 1938. In the 1998 flood, 1,562 people lost their lives (compared with 1.4 million in the 1911 flood), most from debris flows in mountain regions. A total of 81,853 square miles (21,200,000 hectares) of land was flooded, with an estimated economic loss of RMB 166.6 billion (US $20.5 billion) (Zong and Chen, 2000).

Anticipation

The Changjiang (Yangtze) Water Resource Commission (CWRC) has had responsibility for flood control of the Yangtze basin for decades, dating back to a 1959 systematic plan for flood control (Ministry of Water Resources, 1999).

In January 1998 (before the 1998 flood occurred), the Chinese government established the first national law for flood prevention (Zhang and Wen, 2001). The law both clarified responsibilities among national and local authorities for flood management and established a set of regulations for control. These regulations limit the land that can be reclaimed from water, promote relocating residents of retention basins to safer places, and give the central government authority to decide whether or not to use retention basins (Ministry of Water Resources, 1999).

Part of the law reorganized the responsibilities among different ministries and departments under the State Council (Zhang and Wen, 2001). The function and responsibility of the Ministry of Water Resources (MWR) was adjusted, and the administrative role of the MWR on hydropower development was moved to the State Economic and Trade Commission. Groundwater management, originally under the Ministry of Geology and Mineral Resources, and urban flood control, originally under the Ministry of Construction, were moved to the MWR. The MWR was mandated to take over the responsibility of management of water conservation all over the country. It was to plan, monitor the water environment, and recommend protection measures to the government at different levels. In this way, a chain of command and responsibility for water resource management was put into place that served the region well when the flood occurred later that year.

In view of the unusual climate during the winter months of 1997 and the spring months in 1998, the CWRC undertook in February 1998 a detailed analysis of streamflow and rainfall in the region, taking into account the El Niño effect, ocean and atmospheric circulation patterns, thermal conditions on the Qinghai-Tibet Plateau, and historical trends in streamflow and precipitation. The commission concluded that there would be basinwide heavy flooding in 1998. Additionally, at the beginning of April 1998, the Department of Meteorology predicted heavy flooding in the Yangtze River basin (Ministry of Water Resources, 1999). Based on these early warnings, the Yangtze River region prepared for the flood. The hydrological departments under the CWRC issued by telegram streamflow forecasts for over 30,000 stations and times, and 1,300 precipitation forecasts. The CWRC also made fairly accurate forecasts of several heavy storm floods, transitional weather processes, and the time when water levels would exceed controls at important stations on the main stem of the middle and lower reaches. Moreover, it issued very accurate forecasts for eight floods, which made it possible to forestall disaster and avoid greater losses than the ones that occurred (Ye and Glantz, 2005).

Actuality

Following the prediction of heavy flooding, the MWR and the State Flood Control and Drought Prevention Headquarters organized various meetings and discussions, and additional flood control measures were planned. Several investigation groups were sent to inspect and assist flood control preparations in the provinces along the river. Based on the findings of these groups, the flood control schemes were reevaluated and revised as necessary. The budget for flood control was supplemented to pay for the repair and renovation of a large number of unsafe hydraulic structures, river dikes, reservoirs, and sluice gates. The materials for flood fighting were well stocked. One of the deputy premiers was appointed to lead the flood control activities in the Yangtze basin (Department of International Cooperation and Technology, 2004).

Mitigation of the 1998 flood was the responsibility of the Changjiang (Yangtze) Flood Control and Drought Prevention Headquarters. It and the CWRC were directly overseen by the Central Committee of the Party. Cutting-edge information technologies, which included the meteorological satellite communication systems, the automatic hydrological telemetry systems, the remote-sensing systems, and the satellite positioning systems, played a crucial role in fighting the flood (Academic Divisions of the Chinese Academy of Sciences, 2005). Different government institutions throughout the country all proactively got involved in the flood control effort. Thanks to these early warnings and preparation efforts, emergency rescue and preservation efforts were largely successful. The loss of life was remarkably small compared with previous large floods along the river. Indeed, most of those who perished did not live in the floodplain areas where casualties had previously been highest but instead were victims of mudslides in the elevated regions above the floodplain. The percentage of regional economic assets lost was smaller than in previous floods, although the total economic losses were higher than historical levels because of the magnitude of economic development that had occurred over the past several decades (Wan, 2003).

Aftermath

After the Yangtze flood of 1998, the Chinese government appropriated RMB 10.1 billion (US $1.22 billion) for the implementation of the "Resettlement in the Stricken Areas Project." The Ministry of Civil Affairs was the leading ministry for rehabilitation of villages and towns; the Ministry of Construction was responsible for the village relocation projects and infrastructure works. The latter ministry formulates general guidelines, whereas the specific layout plans for the new villages are prepared at the provincial level by professional planning and design institutes. The government established a policy that recovery efforts should not simply restore the affected areas to their pre-disaster conditions but should aim at improved living conditions for the people and should support complementary development initiatives. Furthermore, reconstruction and rehabilitation should take place in the original location of the settlements whenever possible. Settlement relocation would be considered only in exceptional cases where the original settlement was located in a high-risk area (e.g., lowlands next to a river, or islands in the river, which require major protective embankments that would have significant impact on the natural flow of the water) or in areas to be reclaimed by river channels or lakes (Li, 2000).

By December 1998, the government had already selected the new sites for the villages that were to be relocated because of the flooding. This was done on the basis of regional development plans and detailed site studies. In some cases, the population of villages being abandoned would be integrated into existing villages or towns, expanding the settlement area and upgrading services such as schools and clinics. In other cases, the villages would be relocated to new places. Villages where the inhabitants were expected to continue working on their original farmland were being relocated within a "comfortable distance from the new village to its fields." "Comfortable distance" was considered to be a maximum of three miles (Li, 2000).

After large-scale construction of water works since 1998, the flood control capacity of the main levees in the lower and middle reach of the Yangtze River was improved and will continue to grow. The 2002 floods along the Yangtze River, though of lesser intensity than those of 1998, demonstrated the effectiveness of structural and nonstructural policies and measures to reduce casualties and economic loss (Department of International Cooperation and Technology, 2004).

Compensation for flood damage was in two tiers: a larger one for relocated families and a smaller one for families who remained. For relocated families, compensation was designed to cover a major portion of the costs of constructing 800 square feet of new housing. Compensation was a blend of cash grants, government loan guarantees for building materials, and tax exemptions. The funds were provided in part by the central government and in part by provincial authorities (Ministry of Water Resources, 1999).

After the 1998 flood, the Chinese government explicitly stated as policy that what is important in the cycle of restoration is not to control but to manage water resources. Based on this understanding, the following so-called 32-character policy was formulated after the flood. The 32-character policy consists of eight items, each of which is expressed in four Chinese characters (Wan, 2003). Thus, this is called a 32 (4 × 8)–character policy, which can be roughly translated as follows:

1. Creating mountain forest preserve areas and planting trees
2. Transforming agricultural lands into forests
3. Demolishing dikes to create floodplain water catchment areas
4. Returning agricultural polders to lakes
5. Supplying laid-off laborers for post-flood reconstruction
6. Relocating residents to form new townships
7. Reinforcing key levees
8. Dredging river beds.

This policy has been implemented in several large reconstruction steps (Wan, 2003):

- *Preventing mudslides.* One major reason for China's frequent water disasters is the serious destruction of the ecosystem and environment, not only because of river flooding but also because of mudslides. The middle and upper reaches of the Yangtze River and Yellow River basins suffer from frequent mudslides, which have caused great losses of life and property. To prevent these, a program of projects has been undertaken, including transforming slope fields into terrace fields, creating forest preserves in mountain areas where cutting and gathering wood is forbidden, planting trees, and transforming farmland into forests and grassland on a large scale.
- *Maintaining the flood control policy of "combining storage and release and focusing on release."* The water structural system built during the past 50 years, including such multipurpose water projects as the Gezhouba and Geheyan, can store a large quantity of floodwater, which reduces the pressure on the levees. The ongoing Three Gorges Project will be speeded up as part of this objective. According to the construction schedule, the flood control capacity of the Three Gorges Project will reach nearly 800 billion cubic feet of water when it is completed in 2009.

- *Demolishing polder fields to release floods and converting farmland into lake area.* Based on preliminary statistics, in the 1998 floods, over 2,000 dikes broke in the lower and middle reaches of the Yangtze River. About 11,000 square miles of arable polder land were inundated and 2.53 million people were left homeless. To raise flood discharge absorption capabilities, almost all these polders will not be reconstituted as farmland but instead will be converted back into lakes.

- *Strengthening the development of safety facilities in the flood detention and storage zones.* Yangtze floods are characterized by high peak levels and large volumes. But the discharge capacities of the river courses are limited. So it is an effective measure to utilize flood detention and storage zones to divert and store extra floodwater to ensure safety of key areas. The extant zones suffered from having dense populations, ongoing economic development, and lagging safety facilities, so the policy was first to strengthen the infrastructure to enhance safety. If that failed, high-risk population and economic centers were relocated.

- *Reinforcing stem levees, constructing high-standard levees, and dredging river beds.* The flood of 1998 showed that reinforcing levees and regulating river courses are important measures to raise flood control capacity. The local governments along the river have made detailed arrangements for the following four priorities: rehabilitating destroyed waterworks, treating levee foundations for seepage, preventing breaks in key levee sections, and increasing the height and width of weak levees.

- *Developing better nonstructural flood control systems.* Driven in part by the experience of the 1998 Yangtze floods and in part by a general evolution in thinking about flood protection, China has adopted an approach that includes both structural and nonstructural aspects. The reconstruction in the Yangtze basin includes not only the Three Gorges Dam but the introduction of advanced monitoring and measuring technologies and equipment to rehabilitate hydrological stations and realize automatic data collection so as to raise the quality and speed of hydrological data collection. In the communications area, through wide use of the national public communication network, such technical measures as satellite, microwave, and integrated communications will be adopted to supplement and improve the flood control communication network so as to strengthen its function. In the computer software research and development area, decision support systems will be established for flood control and drought relief at the central, river basin, provincial, and city levels, to improve flood control dispatching and achieve scientific decisionmaking.

Observations

Considered from a water management point of view, the Yangtze River provides close to an ideal case. From anticipation based on previous experience, combined with a commitment to safety, environmental, and economic considerations, plans were formulated. A multilevel integrated water management system has been put into place that reflects learning from previous experience. Modern technology is employed where possible. Of course, all this has occurred within a culture that is accepting of top-down direction and control to an extent that is unacceptable in most Western cultures, much less the American one. The challenge of this case is to find ways of incorporating the desirable elements of water management found here through a system of individual incentives and decentralized government policies. Although this task is difficult, the benefits of achieving it make the effort worthwhile.

CHAPTER THREE

Synthesis of the Lessons from the Case Studies

The four cases that we have examined are all illustrative of the evolution in thinking about flood management that has taken place in the past 60 years and that has led to new ways of thinking about future floods. In this chapter, we proceed through the cycle of restoration to synthesize the lessons learned from the four case studies. In Chapter Four, we present conclusions from this synthesis that apply to the restoration of the Gulf Coast region following Hurricane Katrina.

Planning

The cases show, through both omission and commission, the value of advance planning. Even though our cases were selected because they represented extreme floods within their respective regions—where even planning could not have entirely averted damage—they nevertheless show the advantage of considering potential problems and creating policies to address them. The Yangtze case illustrates this best: The policies and response organization that were put into place paid major dividends when the floodwaters arrived. The Zeeland case also illustrates this from the opposite viewpoint: Ignoring warnings for decades meant that the population was essentially helpless against the onslaught of the storm. Vanport shows that where planning was adequate (i.e., the larger Columbia basin area), mitigation was generally successful, but where planning was inadequate (i.e., Vanport specifically), the effects were disastrous. For the 1993 Mississippi flood, planning based on lessons learned from previous river floods made detection, preparation, and first response better than they otherwise would have been.

Detection

In each of these flood-prone regions, the question was not *whether* flooding will happen but *when* it will happen again. Modern technology has been brought to bear, including satellite weather observation and improved modeling of storm and river flow patterns, as well as communication technology to get word of the threat to those people who are at risk. The Mississippi and Yangtze cases both benefited from use of this technology, and the Zeeland case provided an impetus for aggressively improving detection and communication capabilities. In the Vanport case, detection of rising flood levels was not a problem, but detection of structural weaknesses in the dikes was. Thus, issues remain concerning the monitoring and detection of structural weaknesses, as well as adequate funding of streamflow, weather, and other elements of the monitoring and detection networks. Inadequate monitoring of structural integrity led to the surprising collapse of the railroad dike in the Vanport case and many of the problems in the Mississippi case.

Preparation

If and when detection is adequate, the issue is what to do with the detected information. The four cases show significant differences in this regard. For Vanport, preparation was believed to be adequate, but because the threat was underestimated, that was not the case. For Zeeland, because of the lack of planning, preparation was minimal and damage was maximal. For the Yangtze, preventive steps were taken before the 1998 flood based on experience from previous floods, and these paid off. For the 1993 Mississippi flood, there was significant variation from place to place because different local agencies had different preparation plans.

Here, the lesson is that receipt of timely meteorological and hydrologic information is insufficient unless this information gets into the right hands and is appropriately applied. Opportunities to mitigate losses in response to the information were forgone in each case. Organizations need to be in place, prepared, and trained to act on the information—and to seek additional help when their own resources are stretched too thin. Similarly, communities need to be prepared to receive warnings and calls for evacuation. In short, better preparation is almost always possible as experience is gained, but sometimes governmental and other entities do not have the organizational capabilities and resources to act on the knowledge gained. This is a common difficulty for governments at any level and type; commitments to invest in risk-reducing measures for low-probability, high-consequence events compete with more immediate demands with faster and more visible payoffs.

First Response

First response in all cases is a reflection of the adequacy of the lines of coordination and communication among the different agencies responsible for the response. In Vanport, even though the preparation was minimal, the local agencies responded quickly and adequately to care for the needs of victims and to minimize their harm. Because the event was so highly localized, efforts by state or federal agencies were not required. In Zeeland, national, regional, and local agencies responded as rapidly and as effectively as possible, and rescue and care operations were rapidly in place. In Mississippi, first response was adequate given the intense nature of the flooding. In Yangtze, first response followed the intensive planning, with the consequent minimization of loss of life—1,500 (mostly from mudslides) compared with 1.4 million (mostly from drowning) in 1911—and care of victims.

Reconstruction

Reconstruction efforts in the sense of reestablishing the functions of everyday life were addressed rapidly in all cases except Vanport, where the community was abandoned. In Zeeland, even though the flood and damage were extreme, some flooding was a part of regular experience, and immediate reconstruction posed no noteworthy problems. In Mississippi, reconstruction was a bottom-up phenomenon, with different local communities choosing from a wide variety of reconstruction strategies. In Yangtze, reconstruction followed the planning that had been established.

Whether to reconstruct according to the status quo ante varied from case to case. In Vanport, the city was abandoned. In Zeeland, the communities were reconstructed largely to their former states, but a long program of flood control and management was begun. In Mississippi, most communities were restored to their former states, a small number were partially or completely relocated, and some modifications were made to the flood protection system. In Yangtze, the flood was the occasion to implement planned reforms that involved moving a number of communities and that instigated both planned changes and the preparation for future changes. The extent to which the status quo ante was restored depended largely on the density and size of remaining populations and the political viability of relocating the most vulnerable communities.

Compensation

Compensation was not a major concern in the Zeeland and Yangtze cases; in both, the national government compensated the victims well according to local standards. It was an issue that was never resolved in the Vanport case. The Mississippi case produced an awareness that governmental and private flood protection insurance policies were inadequate, sometimes in the area of not providing adequate protection and sometimes creating a moral hazard where government protection deterred adequate insurance and shifted what perhaps should be a private burden to the public sector. Strong recommendations were made in terms of who should take responsibility for risks and what the relationship of insurance and government compensation after losses should be; these recommendations were, however, not fully implemented (Dixon et al., 2006). These insurance lessons are still being considered in the Netherlands and in China, and they merit fuller consideration in the United States as well.

Learning and Implementing Lessons

The four cases were highly variable in their approach to learning and implementing lessons to plan for the next cycle of restoration. In Vanport, the abandonment of the town led to virtually no searching for lessons to be learned. The larger issue of management of the Columbia River continued according to previous plans, with little or no adjustment resulting from the 1948 experience. For Zeeland, the catastrophe triggered a long-term evolution of thinking.

At first, the thinking was in terms of protection from a repetition of the flood, at almost any cost. However, with time and the innovative potential of technological advancement, Dutch authorities began incorporating environmental and economic factors along with the safety and cultural ones. More recently, the Dutch included the radical step of surrendering land back to the water—unthinkable 60 years ago but under way at the present. Currently, the Dutch think in terms of integrated water resource management, where all tools—stronger levees, surge barriers, early warning systems, insurance reforms, and surrendering land—are candidates for use. The Mississippi flood of 1993 triggered extensive investigations and analyses, with many recommendations for change. However, the implementation of the recommended changes has been uneven. Examples of follow-through on those lessons can be found throughout the United States, but the consensus appears to be that these lessons must be better attended to (see, for example, Davis and Dunning, 2005; Faber, 1997; and Galloway, 2005a,b). Some in the academic community are attempting to understand what is necessary to promote a better understanding of reconstruction, as well as the rest of the cycle (e.g., Kirschenbaum, 2005; Norris-Raynbird, 2005). In the Yangtze, the 1998 event was carefully studied, and further reforms that arose out of the experience were rapidly implemented.

A common trend over the past 60 years has been the evolution from the attempt to control floods to a broader notion of integrated water resource management. This was reflected in some way in all the cases. For Vanport, the brief history and transience of the community led quickly to a decision not to rebuild the city, and a previous focus on the overall management of the Columbia continued to be national policy. Zeeland shows this evolution most clearly, as original plans for enclosing dikes were replaced by the building of storm surge barriers that preserved the economic and ecological characteristics of the region. The Dutch government has shown a willingness to invest in technology and to attend to environmental concerns, at the same time maintaining a focus on a necessary level of safety. The Mississippi case highlighted the long-standing battle in that region (Barry, 1997) between the structural and nonstructural approaches to restoration. By contrast, the Yangtze case shows that if policymakers are willing to learn from experience and have the unimpeded power to implement their lessons, modern management can be effective.

The key actors in implementing integrated water resource management in the United States will continue to include the federal government, especially FEMA (for preparation and response) and the Army Corps of Engineers; state and local governments; and the communities themselves for all aspects of the restoration cycle.

The mandate of FEMA is typically thought of as offering immediate relief to victims; subsequently supporting repairing and rebuilding damaged property after major disasters; and compensating, through relief and insurance, private victims of those disasters. But it also has a mandate to encourage the reduction of risk from disasters, and it can perform this job in a wide variety of ways. As part of its total mandate, FEMA already has the authority it needs to think in terms of flood management by integrating structural and nonstructural aspects of reconstruction and compensation. The question is whether the agency adequately exercises its authority to the fullest extent.

In contrast, the Army Corps of Engineers operates under strict guidance from Congress, which typically favors structural alternatives to more complex integrated management alternatives that may conflict with local land use prerogatives. Although the Corps has long used property buyouts as a tool to reduce risks from flooding, it cannot easily employ that tool on anything but a small scale because of political and financial constraints.

Several overarching lessons can be drawn from the examples:

- *Building bigger and better flood protection works does not necessarily maximize safety.* Surrendering land to the water in the form of forgoing development of floodplains or active removal of formerly reclaimed land can lead to reduction in property loss and lives at risk.
- *Differing perceptions among residents and political leaders of permanence and transience of the physical environment can create conflicts in decisions about what to rebuild, what to modify, and what to leave as is.* In democratic societies, resolution of these differing viewpoints is best accomplished in an open political process—in particular, a broad public discussion about alternatives to the status quo ante. In this discussion, flood control is not the only objective to be considered.
- *Some potential improvements to the status quo ante are not intuitively apparent or politically palatable.* In the absence of analysis, there is an inherent bias toward recreating what used to be. Regional leaders would do well to expend effort designing and analyzing a number of alternative policies following a flood disaster as a foundation for informed public debate and increased public awareness of the options and tradeoffs.
- *Structural solutions are necessary but not sufficient.* Decisionmakers and the public tend to be overconfident about engineering solutions because the solutions appear to offer substantial protection along with economic development benefits. Instead, decisionmakers need to choose structural elements that are compatible with nonstructural approaches intended to achieve a balance with other longer-term economic, environmental, and social objectives. Although this lesson has evolved in the past century from being implicit to being explicit, it is still salient as long as the Army Corps of Engineers continues to play a dominant role in flood management in the United States.

CHAPTER FOUR

Lessons for the Aftermath of Katrina

We undertook this historical analysis to seek insights that might guide current reconstruction efforts in the Gulf Coast region in the aftermath of Hurricane Katrina, which struck in the late summer of 2005. In this concluding chapter, we apply the lessons learned from the four case studies to the current aftermath phase of Katrina. Our aim is to provide guidance for going forward rather than to look backward to cast blame. We will then close with some general observations.

An Overview of Katrina

Katrina's winds, rain, and storm surges—and the failure of multiple levees stressed by the surges—wrought unprecedented death and destruction over a 90,000-square-mile area. Over 1,200 lives were lost. Property losses in Louisiana, Mississippi, and Alabama have been estimated to be between just under $100 billion to as much as $200 billion, with $40–60 billion of those losses insured (White House, 2006; Risk Management Solutions, 2005). As of this writing, temporary housing has been provided for over 700,000 people (GAO, 2006b). Throughout the region, many residents who evacuated before the storm have not yet returned—either by choice or by necessity (McCarthy et al., 2006). Much of the existing housing stock will require significant repair and renovation, and many essential city services have not yet been restored to pre-Katrina levels. Only a few public schools in New Orleans have reopened, and health care is still inadequate for the population even at its current reduced levels (White House, 2006).

Lessons from History

As our examples show, Katrina and its aftermath, like many crises, present an opportunity to improve on conditions that existed prior to the catastrophe. The elements of the cycle of restoration offer a framework to consider lessons that may be relevant to leaders in the Gulf Coast region.

In terms of *planning* and *preparation*, all the examples demonstrate to varying degrees the limits of planning when the natural disaster exceeds expectations. Government officials had anticipated catastrophic flooding in New Orleans from flooding and levee failures. Further, officials also were well aware of the connection between loss of Louisiana's coastal wetlands and reduction in the city's protection from storm surges. On the coasts of the Gulf of Mexico, storm surges had been anticipated, but not at the heights wrought by Katrina (White House, 2006). In the future, regional leaders should consider policies and plans that are more robust against a wider range of disaster scenarios.

Throughout the region, however, the biggest blind spot was the failure to anticipate the possibility of widespread regional breakdown in infrastructure and services and the disabling of first-response and public safety systems. Some activities, such as evacuation planning, simply cannot be implemented on the fly. Evacuation services for all segments of the population must be worked through in sufficient detail well in advance of the event. The fragility of many structures on the Gulf Coast, along with the fact that so many of them were built to out-of-date building codes, underscores another opportunity for improvement. Here, the lessons of history are that, while determining safety levels might be defensible on cost-benefit or IWRM bases, the planning for regional infrastructure and services must cover total catastrophic breakdown and must include secondary, contingency responses that can be invoked when primary responses are overwhelmed. In Zeeland, lack of such planning led to catastrophe, but in the Yangtze case, this planning was a major reason why loss was only a fraction of what had been suffered in previous floods.

At the federal level, much has already been published about the shortcomings of FEMA and other agency planning efforts, particularly in the advanced development of logistics for deploying supplies and personnel (White House, 2006; GAO, 2006b). Although scenario planning had been employed by FEMA, it will need to anticipate a wider range of scenarios in the future to fully prepare its staff for a wider range of catastrophic conditions in major metropolitan areas.

Detection of the storm itself was certainly adequate in the case of Katrina—as it was in the historical examples—but where detection fell short was in anticipating structural failures and collapse under the forces unleashed by the storm. In the case of New Orleans, the Corps and the local levee districts had no monitoring equipment in place to detect structural weaknesses, soil anomalies, and impending failure (American Society of Civil Engineers Assessment Team, 2005; U.S. Army Corps of Engineers, 2006). This is a shortcoming that can be remedied through extensive deployment of sensors on all structural features of the flood protection system.

The examples suggest that decisions about how to proceed with reconstruction in the affected areas are strongly influenced by the answer to the question, What will the level of hurricane protection be in the future? In the four cases examined in this study, that decision was intimately tied to the commitment of the affected population to restore their way of life to pre-disaster conditions, albeit with some accommodation to the natural hazards. The Vanport example offers one extreme: The community was temporary, and residents' emotional ties to it were weak. The Zeeland example is at the opposite end of the continuum: Wholesale abandonment of the flooded lands was simply not an option for a small country, although over time the Dutch became willing to give back some land to the sea in return for more security.

The areas affected by Katrina and its aftermath fall in between these two extremes. By and large, Gulf Coast residents feel a strong connection to these special places, and yet they do have choices of where to live within the United States in ways that the Dutch did not perceive that they had. This psychological difference casts the public decision about the appropriate level of flood protection in more complex terms.

This consideration raises the larger issue of how to deal with the long-term evacuee population we face in Katrina. Of our historical examples, only China needed to consider mass movements of people, and the Chinese solution is not applicable to the United States. Most instances of flooding are short-term in nature—in terms of how long it takes for the floodwaters to recede and how long it is before people can be back in their communities. But Katrina resulted in a situation where there is permanent or semipermanent displacement—more akin to the Chernobyl disaster in Ukraine or what will have to be done in case of a terrorist dirty bomb attack. This is an entirely different class of problem, one that requires possibly pioneering thinking in the restoration of the Gulf region.

Individual and collective decisions about how to proceed with reconstruction in the affected areas of the Gulf Coast are interconnected in complex ways, sometimes referred to in shorthand as the "chicken and egg" problem. Uncertainty about the future level of protection will temper or tip investments and the rebuild/relocate decisions that ultimately shape the scope of reconstruction. Oliver Houck's seminal article "Can We Save New Orleans?" (Houck, 2006) brings these uncertainties about commitment to coastal restoration and level of flood protection into stark relief.

Investments in additional flood control and protective measures will depend on the density and magnitude of populations and property requiring protection. This uncertainty persists in the Gulf coast region even with the release of long-awaited FEMA maps showing revised estimates of vulnerability to flooding. The lessons of Zeeland apply to the situation along the coastline in Alabama, Mississippi, and Louisiana. The Dutch have conscientiously employed the philosophy of IWRM in balancing protection, the environment, and the economic well-being of the population in determining treatment of coastal areas. Their use of technological and political innovation could be fruitfully applied to Mobile, Alabama; Biloxi, Mississippi; St. Bernard Parish, Louisiana; and other seriously damaged coastal areas.

Many Gulf Coast residents have already seized options to move elsewhere within the United States. These options complicate national decisions about the appropriate level of flood protection when population estimates and economic recovery remain uncertain. Under these circumstances, estimates of population return and the quality of a range of locally provided public services become important determinants of the extent to which the federal government should rebuild preexisting levees and improve flood protection through other nonstructural means.

Finally, it is still too soon to tell the full story of compensation in the aftermath of Katrina. Preliminary analysis from FEMA shows that in areas of the disaster zone where it applied, compliance with the National Flood Insurance Program was relatively good. However, the program's coverage is incomplete in the flood-prone areas hit by Katrina. Much could be done to strengthen the market penetration of federally backed flood insurance (Dixon et al., 2006). Beyond the limits of the NFIP, private insurers faced major losses in Katrina (Risk Management Solutions, 2005) and will likely support more robust flood protection measures, reforms in building codes, and enlightened land-use planning that will reduce their exposure in the future, assuming that they choose to continue to serve the region. This issue is clearly an important area for future analysis and policy change.

Final Observations

We close with some general observations that span the cycle of restoration.

- George Santayana (1905) said, "Those who cannot remember the past are condemned to repeat it." This has clearly been shown in our case studies. The Zeeland and Yangtze cases show that attending to the lessons from past flooding leads to an ability to improve on historical outcomes. The Mississippi case shows that not following up on the lessons of past flooding leads to avoidable damages. Attending to history leads to mitigating the potential damage of floods even when major floods are few and far between; ignoring history leads to even larger disasters. Whether the Gulf Coast region will adequately attend to its recent flooding history remains to be seen.
- The critical concept of integrated water resource management policy—particularly its implication that flood control includes conceding land to the water from time to time—is a psychologically and politically difficult one. This is a problem that goes well beyond flood control. In almost all areas of preventive policy, there are times when an excess of cure can be worse than the disease. Increased development induced by structural barriers such as levees often adds to risks from flooding.
- Advanced delineation of roles and responsibilities shapes outcomes. As with any large-scale events, there were many different actors in each flood—national governments, local governments, engineers, the private business sector, and communities. When those actors had well-defined and well-understood roles, things generally went well. However, when such definition and understanding were lacking, the consequences of the disaster were magnified. The flooding of New Orleans shows that this lesson has yet to be fully absorbed for disasters in which local capacity is overwhelmed and the impacts are regional in their scope.
- Out of tragedy can come opportunity. In each of the cases, there were improvements to the social and physical infrastructure in the reconstruction phase that went beyond flood protection. This shows that disruption of the status quo can create political conditions for broader-based social and economic change that might otherwise have been delayed or not happened at all. It is still too soon to tell whether this latest cycle of restoration in the Gulf Coast region will lead upward or downward.

In sum, the cases provide a sufficiently diverse set of circumstances from which to draw useful similarities and contrasts to the current situation in the Gulf. While social, economic, environmental, and political conditions before the disaster provide the stage and the props for the post-disaster response and reconstruction efforts, the cases clearly show that the past need not be prologue.

Bibliography

Academic Divisions of the Chinese Academy of Sciences (2005). "Thoughts about the 1998 Yangtze river flood and suggestions for future work (in Chinese)." Available at http://www.casad.ac.cn/2005-5/20055992258.htm, accessed 13 January 2006.

American Red Cross, Portland-Multnomah County Chapter (1948). *Vanport City Flood, May 30, 1948: Preliminary Disaster Committee Report.* Portland, OR: Archive document accessed at Central Library, Portland.

American Society of Civil Engineers Assessment Team (2005). *Preliminary Report on the Performance of the New Orleans Levee Systems in Hurricane Katrina on August 29, 2005.* Report No. UCB/CITRIS–05/01, 17 November 2005. Available at http://www.asce.org/files/pdf/katrina/team datareport1121.pdf, accessed 7 June 2006.

Arend, M. (1993). "Strong balance sheets ease flood effects." *American Bankers Association Banking Journal,* Vol. 85, p. 11.

Associated Press (2002). "2002 floods not as bad, thanks to improvements after '93." 19 May.

Axelrod, C., P. P. Killam, M. H. Gaston, and N. Stinson (1994). "Primary health care and the Midwest flood disaster." *Public Health Report,* Vol. 109, pp. 601–605.

Barry, J. M. (1997). *Rising Tide: The Great Mississippi Flood of 1927 and How It Changed America.* New York: Touchstone.

Bhowmilk, N. G. (1996). "Physical effects: Positive and negative outcomes." In S. A. Changnon, ed., *The Great Flood of 1993: Causes, Impacts and Responses,* New York: Westview Press, pp. 101–131.

Bonneville Power Administration (2001). *The Columbia River System Inside Story,* second edition. Portland, OR.

———— (no date). "NW Hydro Flood Control." Available at http://www.bpa.gov/Power/pl/columbia/2-flood.htm, accessed 11 January 2006.

Buss, D. (1993). "Flood effects ripple beyond Midwest." *Restaurant Business,* Vol. 92, p. 21.

Buss, L. S. (2005). "Nonstructural flood damage reduction within the U.S. Army Corps of Engineers." *Journal of Contemporary Water Research & Education,* No. 130, pp. 26–30.

Cartwright, L. (2005). "An examination of flood damage data trends in the United States." *Journal of Contemporary Water Research & Education,* No. 130, pp. 20–25.

Center for Columbia River History (no date). "The Flood: Floating 'like corks.' " Portland, OR. Available at http://www.ccrh.org/comm/slough/vpflood.htm, accessed 11 January 2006.

Changnon, S. A. (1996a). "Defining the flood: A chronology of key events." In S. A. Changnon, ed., *The Great Flood of 1993: Causes, Impacts and Responses*, New York: Westview Press, pp. 3–28.

——— (1996b). "Impacts on transportation systems: Stalled barges, blocked railroads, and closed highways." In S. A. Changnon, ed., *The Great Flood of 1993: Causes, Impacts and Responses*, New York: Westview Press, pp. 183–204.

——— (1996c). "Losers and winners: A summary of the flood's impacts." In S. A. Changnon, ed., *The Great Flood of 1993: Causes, Impacts and Responses*, New York: Westview Press, pp. 276–299.

——— (2005). "The 1993 flood's aftermath: Risks, root causes, and lessons for the future." *Journal of Contemporary Water Research & Education*, No. 130, pp. 70–74.

Clement, D. (2001a). "Out of harm's way." *Fedgazette*, Vol. 13, September, p. 5. Available at http://www.minneapolisfed.org/pubs/fedgaz/01-09/control.cfm?js=0, accessed 10 January 2006.

——— (2001b). "Dam it all!" *Fedgazette*, Vol. 13, September, p. 6. Available at http://www.minneapolisfed.org/pubs/fedgaz/01-09/control.cfm?js=0, accessed 10 January 2006.

——— (2001c). "The failure of flood control," *Fedgazette*, Vol. 13, November, p. 6. Available at http://www.minneapolisfed.org/pubs/fedgaz/01-09/control.cfm?js=0, accessed 10 January 2006.

Cooperative Program on Water and Climate (no date). "Coping with water and climate change in the Netherlands." Available at http://www.waterandclimate.org/dialogue/documents/Factsheet%20NL%20website.pdf, accessed 5 June 2006.

Dantzig, D. van (1956). "Economic decision problems for flood prevention." *Econometrica*, Vol. 24, No. 3, July, pp. 276–287. Available at http://www.jstor.org/view/00129682/di952530/95p0075h/0, accessed 8 February 2006.

Darlin, D. (1995). "A new flavor of pork." *Forbes*, Vol. 155, 5 June, p. 146.

Davis, A. A., and M. C. Dunning (eds.) (2005). Special issue on "Flood first response since the great Midwest flood of 1993." *Journal of Contemporary Water Research and Education*, No. 130, March.

DeClark, L. M. (1997). "Flood insurance helps manage risk of financial loss." Community Dividend. Available at http://minneapolisfed.org/pubs/cd/97f-w/flood-ins.cfm, accessed 9 January 2006.

Deltawerken (no date [a]). "Climatic Circumstances." Available at http://www.deltawerken.com/Climatic-circumstances/483.html, accessed 8 February 2006.

——— (no date [b]). "Rescues and Consequences." Available at http://www.deltawerken.com/Rescue-and-consequences/309.html, accessed 8 February 2006.

——— (no date [c]). "Before the Flood." Available at http://www.deltawerken.com/Before-the-flood-of-1953/90.html, accessed 8 February 2006.

——— (no date [d]). "Devastating Power of the Sea." Available at http://www.deltawerken.com/Devastating-Powers/484.html, accessed 8 February 2006.

Department of International Cooperation and Technology, Ministry of Water Resources (People's Republic of China) (2004). "Flood prevention and management in China [in Chinese]." Available at http://www.cws.net.cn/gpwyh/fhygl/ArticleView.asp?ArticleID=No&ClassID=1514, accessed 10 January 2006.

Dialogue on Water and Climate (2002). "Coping with water and climate change in the Netherlands." Available at http://www.waterandclimate.org/dialogue/documents/Factsheet%20NL%20website.pdf, accessed 30 March 2006.

Dixon, L., N. Clancy, S. A. Seabury, and A. Overton (2006). *The National Flood Insurance Program's Market Penetration Rate: Estimates and Policy Implications.* Santa Monica, CA: RAND Corporation, TR-300-FEMA.

Economist (1993). "And the waters prevailed (1993 Midwestern flood, American survey)." Vol. 328, No. 7820, 17 July, p. A23.

Environmental Protection Agency (no date [a]). "The Mississippi River Basin and Gulf of Mexico Hypoxia: Culture/History." Available at http://www.epa.gov/msbasin/culture.htm, accessed 14 February 2006.

———— (no date [b]). "The Mississippi River Basin and Gulf of Mexico Hypoxia: Subbasins and Gulf." Available at http://www.epa.gov/msbasin/subbasins/index.htm, accessed 14 February 2006.

Faber, S., ed. (1997). Special issue on "Flood policy and management: A post-Galloway progress report." *River Voices,* Vol. 8, No. 2, Summer.

Federal Emergency Management Agency (no date). "This is FEMA." Available at http://www.fema.gov/pdf/library/thisisfema.pdf, accessed 18 February 2006.

Fletcher, M., and M. E. Pflum (1993a). "Few flood losses insured." *Business Insurance,* 19 July.

———— (1993b). "Insured losses rising." *Business Insurance,* 19 July.

Galloway, G. E., Jr. (2005a). "Corps of Engineers response to the changing national approach to floodplain management since the 1993 Midwest flood." *Journal of Contemporary Water Research & Education,* No. 130, pp. 5–12.

———— (2005b). "Statement to the Committee on Transportation and Infrastructure, Subcommittee on Water Resources and the Environment, U.S. House of Representatives, October 27, 2005."

———— (no date). "Floodplain management: A present and a 21st century imperative." Available at http://www.ucowr.siu.edu/updates/pdf/V97_A2.pdf, accessed 14 February 2006.

GAO—*See* Government Accountability Office.

George, C., E. Washington, and M. McGregor (2005). "The Vanport flood." Radio broadcast by the Oregon Historical Society, 16 September 2005. Available at http://www.opb.org/programs/oregon-territory/episodes/2005/0916/, accessed 10 January 2006.

Goeller, B. F., A. F. Abrahamse, J. G. Bolten, D. M. de Ferranti, J. C. De Haven, T. F. Kirkwood, and R. Petruschell (1977). *Protecting an Estuary from Floods—A Policy Analysis of the Oosterschelde.* Vol. I, *Summary Report.* Santa Monica, CA: RAND Corporation, R-2121/1-NETH.

Government Accountability Office (2005). *Hurricane Protection: Statutory and Regulatory Framework for Levee Maintenance and Emergency Response for the Lake Pontchartrain Project.* Washington, DC: GAO-06-322T, 15 December.

———— (2006a). *Federal Emergency Management Agency: Challenges for the National Flood Insurance Program,* Washington, DC: GAO-06-335T, 25 January.

———— (2006b). *Hurricane Katrina: GAO's Preliminary Observations Regarding Preparedness, Response, and Recovery,* Washington, DC: GAO-06-442T, 8 March.

Greenberg, K. E., and A. Shell (1993). "Keeping business afloat during a disaster." *Public Relations Journal,* Vol. 49, No. 9, p. 6.

Hananel, S. (2005). "New developments rise in flood plain, despite risks." Associated Press, 7 April.

Hoogheemraadschap van Delfland (2006). "Projecten ABCDelfland, Oversicht 2006 [ABCDelfland projects, 2006 oversight]." Available at http://www.hhdelfland.nl/contents/pages/9327/hhdprojectenboek2006lr.pdf, accessed 30 March 2006.

Houck, Oliver (2006). "Can we save New Orleans?" *Tulane Environmental Law Journal*, Vol. 19, No. 1, Spring, pp. 1–68.

IFMRC—*See* Interagency Floodplain Management Review Committee.

Interagency Floodplain Management Review Committee (1994). *Sharing the Challenge: Floodplain Management into the 21st Century.* Report to the Administration Floodplain Management Task Force. Washington, DC: U.S. Government Printing Office.

Jackson, Brian, et al. (2002). *Protecting Emergency Responders: Lessons Learned from Terrorist Attacks.* Santa Monica, CA: RAND Corporation, CF-176-OSTP.

Kirschenbaum, A. (2005). "Preparing for the inevitable: Environmental risk perceptions and disaster preparedness." *International Journal of Mass Emergencies and Disasters*, Vol. 23, pp. 97–127.

Koellner, W. H. (1996). "Flood hydrology." In S. A. Changnon, ed., *The Great Flood of 1993: Causes, Impacts and Responses*, New York: Westview Press, pp. 68–100.

Kok, M., J. K. Vrijling, P.H.A.J.M. van Gelder, and M. P. Vogelsang (2002). "Risk of flooding and insurance in the Netherlands." *Proceedings of the Second International Symposium on Flood Defense (ISFD 2002), Beijing, 10–13 September.* Beijing: HKV Publications.

Li, Antian, Changjiang (Yangtze) Water Resources Commission, People's Republic of China (2000). "The 1998 Yangtze river flood and the regulation of the River [in Chinese]." Available at http://www.cjw.com.cn/index/leader/detail/20041212/14969.asp, accessed 3 January 2006.

Loven, J. (1998). "Government to cut off those frequently wiped out by floods." Associated Press, 30 November.

Maben, M. (1987). *Vanport.* Portland, OR: Oregon Historical Society.

McCarthy, Kevin F., D. J. Peterson, Narayan Sastry, and Michael Pollard (2006). *The Repopulation of New Orleans After Hurricane Katrina.* Santa Monica, CA: RAND Corporation, TR-369-RC.

McManamy, R. (1993a). "Midwest floods just keep swelling." *Engineering News-Record*, Vol. 231, No. 3, p. 8.

———— (1993b). "Corps finds itself in middle of a heated policy debate." *Engineering News-Record*, Vol. 231, No. 4, p. 14.

McManamy, R., S. W. Setzer, and T. Ichniowski (1993). "Midwest goes into repair mode," *Engineering News-Record*, Vol. 231, No. 6, p. 8.

Ministry of Transport, Public Works and Water Management [the Netherlands] (2000). *A Different Approach to Water: Water Management Policy in the 21st Century.* The Hague.

———— (2001). *The Delta Project for Safety, Wildlife, Space, and Water.* The Hague.

Ministry of Water Resources (People's Republic of China) (1999). "The 1998 Great Flood in China [in Chinese]." Available at http://www.cws.net.cn/98flood/index.html/, accessed 2 January 2006.

Monteverde, G. (1997). "Some history about the Portland area levees (dikes): Holding back the waters— The U.S. Army Corps of Engineers and flood control along the lower Columbia." *Freshwater News*, April.

Nixon, M. (2005). "Business risks in floodplain navigate commercial drive." *St. Louis Daily Record/St. Louis Countian*, 14 May.

Norris-Raynbird, C. (2005). "A mitigation tale of two Texas cities." *International Journal of Mass Emergencies and Disasters*, Vol. 23, pp. 37–73.

Olsthoorn, A. A., and R.S.J. Tol (2001). *Floods, Flood Management and Climate Change in the Netherlands*. Amsterdam: Institute for Environmental Studies (IVM), Vrije Universiteit.

O'Neil, T. (2003). "Great flood eclipsed all records." *St. Louis Post-Dispatch*, 14 December.

Rebuffoni, D. (1995). "Flood of '93 is having ecological ripple effect." *Star Tribune* (Minneapolis), 13 March.

Risk Management Solutions (2005). *Hurricane Katrina: Profile of a Super Cat*. Newark, CA. Available at http://www.rms.com/Publications/KatrinaReport_LessonsandImplications.pdf, accessed 5 June 2006.

St. Louis Post-Dispatch (2004). "High water mark." 9 March.

Santayana, George (1905/1998). *The Life of Reason*. Amherst, NY: Prometheus Books.

Scanlon, J. (2005). "Strange bed partners: Thoughts on the London bombings of July 2005 and the link with the Indian Ocean tsunami of December 26th 2004." *International Journal of Mass Emergencies and Disasters*, Vol. 23, pp. 149–158.

Taylor, B. (2001). "Lessons from last floods hold water today." Associated Press, 20 April.

———— (2003). "Development thrives as Chesterfield banks on levee protection." Associated Press, 29 May.

Towle, F. I. (no date). *Vanport Flood, 1948*. Engineering investigator's notebook. Archive document accessed at Central Library, Portland, OR.

Truman, Harry S (1948). "President Harry Truman Visits the Portland Civic Auditorium in the Aftermath of the Vanport Flood." Speech given in June 1948. Available at http://www.ccrh.org/comm/slough/oral/trumanspch.htm, accessed 10 January 2006.

University Park Community Center (no date). "The History of Vanport." Portland, OR: Portland State University. Available at http://www.universitypark.org/vanport/, accessed 11 January 2006.

U.S. Army Corps of Engineers (no date). "The great flood of 1993 post-flood report." Available at http://www.mvr.usace.army.mil/PublicAffairsOffice/HistoricArchives/Floodof1993/pafr.htm, accessed 15 February 2006.

U.S. Army Corps of Engineers, Interagency Performance Evaluation Taskforce (2006). *Draft Final Report*, Vol. I (Executive Summary) and eight additional volumes of technical information, 1 June. Available at https://ipet.wes.army.mil/, accessed 7 June 2006.

U.S. Geological Survey (USGS) (no date[a]). "The great flood of 1993." Available at http://mo.water.usgs.gov/Reports/1993-Flood/, accessed 15 February 2006.

———— (no date [b]). "Stream gauging and flood forecasting." Available at http://water.usgs.gov/wid/FS_209-95/mason-weiger.html#HDR3, accessed 15 February 2006.

Ven, G.P. van de, ed. (1992). *Man-Made Lowlands: History of Water Management and Land Reclamation in the Netherlands*. Utrecht: Matrijs.

Verhagen, H. J. (2000). *Organization of Flood Defense in The Netherlands*. Delft, Netherlands,: UNESCO-IHE Institute for Water Education, IHE-Delft, 17 April.

Wan, Hongtao (2003). "Policies and measures on flood mitigation in China since 1998." *International Conference on Total Disaster Risk Management, 2–4 December 2003*. Available at http://www.adrc. or.jp/publications/TDRM2003Dec/11_MR.%20HONGTAO%20WAN%20_FINAL_.pdf, accessed 2 January 2006.

Welkins, L. (1996). "Living with the flood: Human and governmental responses to real and symbolic risk." In S. A. Changnon, ed., *The Great Flood of 1993: Causes, Impacts and Responses*, New York: Westview Press, pp. 218–244.

White House (2006). *The Federal Response to Hurricane Katrina: Lessons Learned*. Washington, DC: Office of the President of the United States.

Witt, J. L. (2005). "Have we learned nothing? Plans for a new levee at St. Peters defy the lessons of the 1993 flood." *St. Louis Post-Dispatch*, 22 April.

Working Group for Post-Hurricane Planning for the Louisiana Coast (2006). *A New Framework for Planning the Future of Coastal Louisiana After the Hurricanes of 2005*. Cambridge, MD: University of Maryland Center for Environmental Science.

Wright, J. M. (1996). "Effects of the flood on national policy: Some achievements, major challenges remain." In S. A. Changnon, ed., *The Great Flood of 1993: Causes, Impacts and Responses*, New York: Westview Press, pp. 245–275.

Ye, Qian, and M. H. Glantz (2005). "The 1998 Yangtze floods: The use of short-term forecasts in the context of seasonal to interannual water resource management." *Mitigation and Adaptation Strategies for Global Change*, Vol. 10, pp. 159–182.

Zhang, Hai-Lun, and Kang Wen (2001). "Flood control and management for large rivers in China." Paper presented at the Workshop on Strengthening Capacity in Participatory Planning and Management for Flood Mitigation and Preparedness in Large River Basins, Bangkok, Thailand, 20–23 November 2001.

Zong, Yongqiang, and Xiqing Chen (2000). "The 1998 flood on the Yangtze, China." *Natural Hazards*, Vol. 22, pp. 165–184.